INCOME ON DEMAND

INCOME

ON DEMAND

Master Your Retirement Portfolio,
Ignore the Market,
and Leave the IRS Weeping

JONATHAN D. BIRD, CFP®

LIONCREST

PUBLISHING

INCOME ON DEMAND

Master Your Retirement Portfolio, Ignore the Market, and Leave the IRS Weeping

ISBN   978-1-5445-0867-2 *Hardcover*

978-1-5445-0866-5 *Paperback*

978-1-5445-0865-8 *Ebook*

CONTENTS

"I'm looking forward to the ugly smell of old books and the sweet smell of good thinking."

FROM EAST OF EDEN, BY JOHN STEINBECK

INTRODUCTION

IN 2018, AMAZON FOUNDER JEFF BEZOS BECAME THE richest person in history, according to one accounting. But in one important way, he is no different than you or me. Every year, he wants income for his personal use—just as we do. Granted, his ambitions are different than ours. Each year, Bezos funds his rocket company to the tune of one billion dollars. He buys big houses, hundreds of thousands of acres, even a nationally prominent newspaper—*The Washington Post*—and any other great stuff that catches his eye.

The first thing to know about his finances, however, is that he does not pay for any of those remarkable things by taking a big salary. His Amazon paycheck hasn't budged from $81,840 a year for the last twenty years. No raises for the guy who started it all!

The second thing to know—and the crucial one, for the

approach to funding retirement I present in this book—is that he is *not* getting that income by having Amazon declare a dividend for its shareholders, which he could easily do. If he did, every one of his shareholders—perhaps you are one of them—would get an Amazon dividend check each and every quarter. Because Bezos is by far Amazon's largest shareholder, he would get by far the biggest dividend. But he did not take that path, for very sound reasons: It could have slowed the growth of his company and lowered the value of Amazon shares each time the company paid out dividends. It could also have imposed income on shareholders who had no desire for it—and collectively cost them millions in taxes. Instead, each and every year, Bezos directs Amazon to reinvest all its cash into new opportunities to grow the business. As the value of the business grows, the stock price tends to appreciate with it. That leaves Bezos in a great position. When he needs income, he simply sells shares of Amazon.

The graphic below shows the effect of his income strategy on his personal holdings over the past twenty years. He went from holding 117 million shares of Amazon to holding 57.5 million shares—a reduction of more than 50 percent. Yet at the same time, the value of his investment in Amazon went from $1.8 billion to over $100 billion.

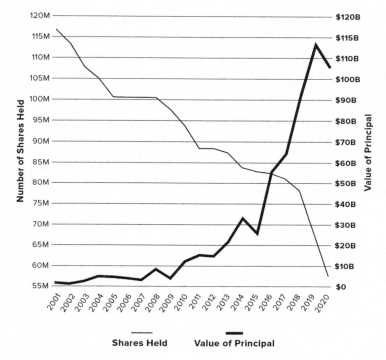

Bezos's Shares Held vs. Value of Principal

Data source: SEC Edgar Database

To say this approach has worked well is a spectacular under-statement. Look at the benefits he's getting from this strategy:

1. He has total control over how much income he takes and when he takes it;
2. He pays less taxes than he would if he received the same income by dividends; and
3. Despite selling shares, his principal is growing exponentially.

You might ask, how is all this possible? The answer: **The price of his stock is appreciating at a faster rate than he is selling shares.** In 2001 Amazon sold for $15.56 a share. When trading closed on Dec. 31, 2019, it sold for $1,847 a share. The stock was appreciating at 28.5 percent per year. At the same time, Bezos was selling about 3.7 percent of his stock per year. So, in spite of selling billions of dollars in Amazon stock, the value of his investment in the company continues to grow and grow. His ownership percentage of the business goes down every year, but the value of his principal continues to go up.

Before I continue, let me assure you I am not writing this book for—or about—billionaires. But I am going to start with billionaires, because the principles they use to handle their finances can inform you about how to handle yours.

NOT JUST FOR BILLIONAIRES

Bezos is not the only billionaire to fund his lifestyle this way. In January of 2010, Larry Page and Sergei Brin, the founders of Google, disclosed plans to sell five million shares apiece over the following five years because like Amazon, Google pays no dividends. Let's look at Larry Page as an example. You might think well, okay, he's selling off about 17 percent of his holdings, so he may be reducing his principal and the value of his holdings. But let's see what happened:

- Holdings as of January 2010: 29.1 million shares at $550 price per share, for a value of $16 billion
- Holdings as of January 2015: 24.1 million shares at $1,084 price per share, for a value of $26.1 billion

So what happened in these five years? First, Page generated roughly $3.5 billion in income by selling 3.4 percent of his stock per year. Second, the value of his principal *increased* by 63 percent, adding an additional $10 billion to his net worth! He didn't lose ground, he gained it. And just like Bezos, he's getting the income he needs simply by selling shares.

Mark Benioff, the founder of Salesforce, takes the same approach, with much the same result. Salesforce has never paid a dividend. When he needs income, he sells shares of his company. But he's selling from growth, and his total holdings are worth more over time because, you guessed it, his stock price is appreciating faster than he is selling shares. He takes income when he needs it, keeps his taxes down versus taking dividends—and indulges his interests. In 2018, Benioff bought *Time* magazine for $190 million with cash from proceeds of stock sales—the same way Bezos laid down $250 million to buy the *Washington Post* five years before.

These billionaires practice taking "income on demand." If you are nearing retirement, or are already there, and if a combination of good work and good fortune has left you with assets of $1 million or more, you can do the same in your retirement—sell from the appreciation in the value of your assets to get income only when you want it. The power of this approach isn't limited to a handful of billionaires. You can apply the same principle that's worked for them to your own portfolio and receive the same benefits. The dollar values these billionaires are taking may be far larger than yours, but the principle of "income on demand" is the same.

This is not a new approach, and I did not invent it. Nor is it a radical strategy. And yet it is not commonly followed. The status quo, the road more often taken, is a dividend-based strategy: focusing on investments that pay dividends now and are expected to continue increasing those dividends in the future. While a dividend-based strategy may be easier for financial advisors to sell to investors, that doesn't mean it will deliver better results. It's like the tale of the fisherman who goes to the local store for bait. The fisherman notices a glittery lure for sale. "Hey mister," he asks the shopkeeper, "do fish really go for this lure?" The shopkeeper looks up at the fisherman and says, "Mister, I don't sell to fish."

In the pages to come, I will demonstrate the drawbacks of the dividend-based approach and the strengths of the total-return strategy I advocate—one that generates returns more from price appreciation than from dividend income.

I will also unfold a way of thinking—and a series of decisions—that can set you up for success with an income-on-demand strategy. My goal is to offer three primary benefits:

First, help you earn more money for yourself and your beneficiaries. I will illustrate how investing your assets in index funds can help minimize the fees you pay and better align your returns with the overall market. This is important! While the overall market (as reflected in the S&P 500) over the past fifty years has returned roughly 10 percent per year with dividends reinvested, investors as a whole have not received that 10 percent due to fees, manager underperformance, and unnecessary taxes.

Second, reduce your tax bill. The income-on-demand strategy may significantly reduce your tax bill compared to the traditional dividends-based strategy. I will also demonstrate how positioning your assets in the right way and drawing on them in the right order can help minimize your taxes—potentially saving up to 1.85 percent of your portfolio value per year.

Third, provide you with peace of mind. I will help you gain confidence in your future through creating a financial plan. I will also help you overcome fear and anxiety about market downturns by sharing four key strategies for maintaining peace of mind through all markets.

FROM FAIRWAY TO FINANCE

I don't come from a family of financiers. I graduated from a Jesuit high school, Brophy College Prep, in Phoenix, Arizona, and went on to attend a Jesuit college, Creighton University in Omaha, Nebraska. I mention my education not because it made me a financial advisor—I graduated from Creighton with a degree in philosophy. Instead, I mention it because my philosophy degree taught me how to think—specifically about the power of "why" questions that other people don't ask.

That habit of thinking didn't lead me directly into finance either. When I graduated from Creighton in 2010, the economy was in the tank. We were mired in the midst of the Great Recession, and I needed a job.

One day my father phoned with a suggestion. "JD," he said—my middle name is David—"I just took this trip to a golf resort called Bandon Dunes. That might be a great place to work." My dad had taught me the game of golf as I grew up. I took his advice. I made the call—and they hired me as a caddy.

The Bandon Dunes Golf Resort sits on a rugged stretch of the southern coast of Oregon that you might mistake for Scotland: rolling, grassy dunes that drop abruptly to the sea. I would carry one or two golf bags at a time for one or two rounds every day with golfers who were there to lose themselves in the beauty and the game. My job was to tell them what club to hit, where to hit their putt, and how to get the most enjoyment out of the course.

One day someone posted a flyer in the caddy shack—yes, we had a caddy shack, just like the movie. Sign your name here, the sign said, if you want to caddy in New Zealand. I scoffed. "Why would I want to go to New Zealand?" I said. Fortunately for me, my buddy Dave was standing nearby. "This is a no-brainer," he said. "Write your name down immediately. Just do it."

To my surprise I got an interview—and the job. Only then did I learn who I'd be working for—Julian Robertson, the hedge fund billionaire—and where: at Kauri Cliffs, a golf resort he developed on the eastern shore of New Zealand. It's ranked thirty-seventh in the world by *Golf Digest*. "He's going to fly you out," they told me. "He's going to pay for you to live there, on the resort. And you're going to work for him."

That sounded good.

In January of 2011 I arrived in New Zealand, unpacked in my lodgings on the sheep farm—and spent a year working as Julian's caddy. Words cannot begin to describe the course's dramatic, seaside beauty. We walked and we talked. I listened as Julian shared remarkable stories of the clients he had helped become millionaires, and then ten times over millionaires—changing lives for the better. I thought, if I could have a fraction of that impact for my own clients, that would be so rewarding and fulfilling.

I began asking questions. Julian's answers were my introduction to the world of finance and investing—a world I had never given any thought to entering before. I had so much to learn. I did not know where to begin.

"JD," Julian told me, in his soft North Carolina accent, "I've got this friend, Warren Buffett. He's great. You should really read his letters."

Buffett, of course, is the chairman and CEO of the legendary investment firm Berkshire Hathaway. By one recent tally, he is the third-wealthiest person in the world. Every year he writes a public letter in which he provides updates to shareholders on the business. He also explains his investment philosophy and insights about various topics. They are all posted on the Berkshire Hathaway website. I've read each one of them more times than I care to admit.

Buffett's letters caused fireworks to go off in my brain. Buffett is an inspiring man. So is his business partner, Charlie Munger. They opened my mind to a world of finance and investing. Their investment philosophy was so simple and powerful that I connected with it in a way that I had not connected with any other subject before. It wasn't only that he had made himself wealthy through his work; he had made his investors wealthier too. Most importantly, he has committed to giving away 99 percent of his wealth to charity. Like Julian, he had made life better for others— many others.

As the prospect of my life's calling, I found that thrilling.

I called my parents after I finished reading. "You guys will never believe what I'm learning from this," I told them. "I value these letters more than my college degree." (I'm sure my dad was thinking, *maybe that's because you majored in philosophy...*)

I had enjoyed an idyllic year carrying golf bags along the gorgeous cliffs of New Zealand. After reading Buffett's letters, I was ready to pack my own bags, make the long flight home, and dig in.

TO SCHWAB—AND BEYOND

At this point, I knew I wanted to work in the field of finance. I knew where I wanted to go—but I did not have the experience I needed to get there. Because I did not already have a formal education in the field, I started by doing research—asking why—to educate myself more fully. And I started looking for advisory firms that embraced the same philosophy as Buffett. This was 2012. Eventually I developed a short list of firms I judged to be doing a reasonable job. I began writing them letters. "I'm Jonathan," each one said. "I believe in value investing and I'm looking for work experience. I will work for you for free."

I got the one letter back that I needed, from Mraz Amerine & Associates in Modesto, California. I worked for them for four months, taking my pay in learning instead of dollars. Mraz Amerine uses Charles Schwab as the custodian for their clients' investment accounts. They suggested that if I wanted to get licensed and formalize my education in the industry, Schwab would be a great place to start.

I moved back home to Phoenix, where about three thousand people work in the Schwab office. In January of 2014, I joined them. I started at ground zero, as a customer service representative. Within six months, I passed the Series 7 and Series 63 exams required to become a registered stockbroker. Then I began placing unsolicited trades for clients who called in with orders.

After a year at Schwab, I was promoted to the high net worth team, where I served clients who held more than one million dollars with Schwab. In my third year, I was promoted to the associate level at Schwab's advisory subsidiary, Schwab Private Client. Before long I became a senior associate, working with an advisor who managed $700 million in assets.

In September of 2017 I was promoted to the advisor role myself. I worked with my own clients—developing their financial plans, creating their portfolios, and helping with their ongoing needs. By 2019, I was working with two hundred high net worth families representing over $250 million in assets. I developed my knowledge and credentials along the way, studying for months as I prepared for the seven-hour test required to become a Certified Financial Planner™. Today the CFP® designation is considered a standard of credibility for investment advisors.

By October of 2019, I had reached the limits of my role with Schwab. I had begun to see the positive impact of the income-on-demand strategy. That was especially true for my retiree clients. I had also begun to see the positive impact my advice was having for clients around how to have financial peace of mind. I wanted to start sharing these ideas and create a positive impact on the wider world.

It was time to take the next step.

BUILDING RETIREMENT CASTLES

Later that fall I opened my own registered investment advisory firm in Phoenix. I named it Farnam Financial.

It's named after Farnam Street in Omaha, where Berkshire Hathaway is run—a tip of the cap to the two men who inspired me. My company logo—a castle turret—captures my goal as a fiduciary to clients: I'm trying to turn every client's financial house into a financial castle.

Just as a castle can stand for protection and longevity, I work to construct portfolios that help protect clients through downturns and provide for them throughout their lifetime. A castle offers both real and psychological protection to its inhabitants. My goal is for the philosophy and strategies inside this book to help provide you with similar protections.

In this book, I offer you a similar service to one I offer my clients: a how-to guide for building your retirement castle, through a plan-based financial future that will generate growth and income for you and your beneficiaries.

This isn't an argument against anything, or a choose-your-side matter of right and wrong. If you are already committed to your way of doing things—and it's working for you—that is great. If the approach you have taken is delivering the retirement you want, then you can set this book down. But if you are curious, anxious, or just a born learner, I hope you will read on. I urge you to read with your own questions in mind—in the same spirit of inquiry that led me to the approach I will lay out in the pages to come. Rather than asking if everything in the book is right or wrong, I hope you'll ask, what parts of this book could be helpful to me? How can I apply its principles to my own financial life in a way that will be obviously useful?

The retirement castle you're building is yours, not mine. I ask only that you take from the book what makes sense to you—and start building!

IF YOU REMEMBER ONE THING...

You can use the same principle that works for billionaires like Jeff Bezos and Larry Page. If your stock appreciates faster than you sell shares, you can get both tax-efficient income and growth of principal.

CHAPTER ONE

THE DIVIDEND INCOME MYTH

ONE DAY AT SCHWAB, I GOT ON THE PHONE FOR AN introductory meeting with a new client named Charlotte. That's where the Schwab process started: I'd spend an hour getting to know you as a client, exploring where you stand in life, what you're looking for, and how I could help. I'd take into account your preferences: investments you want to keep, industries you favor, industries you want to avoid, and so on. And I'd come back to you with a proposal with changes that I believed were in your best interest.

Twenty percent of Charlotte's portfolio was in ExxonMobil stock, and she made one thing clear: she did not want to touch it.

"Why?" I asked.

"Because it pays such a great dividend," she said.

Charlotte was right. Her stock did pay a good dividend. At the time, ExxonMobil was trading at about $80 a share. It paid $3.48 per share in dividends every year. That worked out to a yield of 4.35 percent. The market as a whole was paying a dividend of 2 percent.

Owning ExxonMobil seemed like a great deal—and once every quarter, Charlotte got a check that reinforced her belief. It felt like free money. Even though she wasn't spending it, she grew accustomed to it, and who wouldn't?

But there was more to the story than that—a bigger picture that I call "the dividend income myth." Dividends are not free money. Understanding why begins with this reality: every time a company pays a quarterly dividend, the value of its stock drops by the same amount. It's an inescapable dynamic.

What's more, while the companies that pay the best dividends stand among the most established and the most familiar, that often means they're the most mature. They frequently don't enjoy the same percentage-growth opportunities that other companies do. As a result, the appreciation of their stock can lag the appreciation of the overall market.

Over the eighteen months after Charlotte and I spoke, ExxonMobil dropped from $80 to below $70 a share. The long-term picture is worse, with shares falling from $83.87 in March of 2015 to $49.96 five years later. The company is still paying its $3.48 dividend per share each year, and as a percentage of the stock price it looks even better than when Charlotte and I spoke—but that's because the stock pricing is falling.

Finally, dividend checks come whether you need the money or not—and if the stock isn't in a retirement account, your dividends are taxable (usually at long-term capital gain tax rates). Take taxes into account, and the performance of dividend-centered stocks against the market as a whole gets worse.

Of course, my point in sharing this story isn't to talk about one particular client or one particular company, but the larger dynamics at play. So, let's turn there. In this chapter, I'll explain how dividends relate to stock price and why companies pay them.

HOW DIVIDENDS WORK

When a company's board of directors decides to pay a dividend, they'll announce it. It's typically done once each quarter. They'll announce how much they're paying, and when. They also set what's called an ex-dividend date: the day the stock will start trading without that dividend. If you buy a stock before the ex-dividend date, you are entitled to receive the upcoming dividend. If you buy it on the ex-dividend day or after, you are not entitled to receive the upcoming dividend.

On that ex-dividend day, when the stock begins trading without the dividend, its opening price will reflect a drop in value of about the same amount as the dividend itself. Market forces that day may affect the price too—but the dividend effect is real, if not exact. The Federal Reserve Bank of Minneapolis studied the subject extensively in the 1990s. Its conclusion: "Over the last several decades, one-for-one marginal price drop has been an excellent (average) rule of thumb."

Here's an example. On May 5, 2017, Costco, the great American wholesale company, closed at \$180.20 a share. On the next trading day, May 8, the company paid a special dividend of \$7 per share. Two days later, on May 10, it paid another dividend of 50 cents per share—for a total of \$7.50 in dividends. The special dividend was a one-time payment, and the smaller one was the company's regular quarterly dividend.

You might think the market would reward a company for paying out \$7.50 by valuing its stock more highly. But from May 5 to May 10 the stock dropped \$8.17 per share, closing at \$172.03 per share on May 10. The \$7.50 in dividends per share had left the stock price and gone into the hands of shareholders.

The reason comes down to what a stock price actually represents. In simplified terms, it can be thought to represent the sum of two figures. First, what the company has the ability to pay in dividends right now from its available cash. Second, what the market believes the company will have the ability to pay in dividends in the future. Not what it will *actually* pay in dividends, but what it will have the *ability* to pay.

That means the relationship between dividends and stock price distills to this: paying a dividend reduces a stock's price because it reduces what the company has the ability to pay in dividends.

Berkshire Hathaway offers a perfect example. It doesn't pay dividends, but the price of its stock is incredibly high: $300,000 for an A share. Why? Because Berkshire Hathaway has the ability to pay extraordinary dividends. As of year-end 2019 it could easily pay out a one-time dividend of $60,000 per A share. It also has the ability to pay out $10,000 per A share in annual dividends. But it doesn't. Therefore, all of that dividend *potential* just keeps accumulating in the stock price.

SAY YOU OWNED A RESTAURANT...

Here's an example to illustrate the connection between stock price and dividends.

Let's say you own a restaurant, and it's doing well. It has $100,000 in cash from past profits sitting in a bank account. Your analysis suggests you can make $50,000 a year going forward. You believe that stream of future profits is worth $500,000 in value today. That means your restaurant's business value is $600,000: $100,000 in cash plus $500,000 in future profits. Think of that business value—$600,000—as the stock price.

If you take $100,000 in cash out of the restaurant as a dividend and put it in your personal account, what happens? The business value of the restaurant just dropped by the same amount. Now the business is worth $500,000.

This is what happens to the stock price when a company pays a dividend!

Remember Charlotte? She kept a close eye on her portfolio and called again one day, concerned.

"JD, my ExxonMobil just dropped," she said. "What's going on?"

It was ex-dividend day, I explained. The company had just paid out its quarterly eighty-seven-cent dividend—and the stock price dropped by eighty-seven cents.

She was taken aback. "If that's true, if the dividend just comes out of price, why are they paying it?"

Great question.

DIVIDENDS ARE A CHOICE

A company isn't required to pay dividends. It's a choice based in the obligation of its business leaders to deliver the best value they can to shareholders. The board of directors and the CEO look at their options for growth and say, "Okay. We're making all this income. What's the most intelligent thing we can do with it?"

If a CEO has opportunities to build new plants or buy other companies and add value, then great. They'll do that. But if they have so much cash that they can't do anything intelligent with some or all of it, and they see no prospects for those opportunities, then they need to return that cash to shareholders so that the shareholders can seek a better return elsewhere. Warren Buffett shared insightful comments on this topic in his letter to shareholders in 1981:

> "What makes sense for the bondholder makes sense for the shareholder. Logically, a company with historic and prospective high returns on equity should retain much or all of its earnings so that shareholders can earn premium returns on enhanced capital. Conversely, low returns on corporate equity would suggest a very

high dividend payout so that owners could direct capital toward more attractive areas. (The Scriptures concur. In the parable of the talents, the two high-earning servants are rewarded with 100 percent retention of earnings and encouraged to expand their operations. However, the non-earning third servant is not only chastised—'wicked and slothful'—but also is required to redirect all of his capital to the top performer. Matthew 25: 14-30)"

Paying dividends is not a sign of weakness. It's a sign of maturity. I've already discussed ExxonMobil. Chevron is another example. Its dividend stands at $5.16 per share per year—but its stock price dropped by 6 percent over the past five years, from $103.55 to $96.55. Chevron isn't defining new markets. It's not transforming life with new products. It's no longer racing after growth. It's paying dividends.

You can't grow a company forever, to infinity and beyond. Companies pay dividends because they don't have the same great reinvestment prospects that they did when they were younger. They're at a different stage in their life cycle.

The technical term underlying the decision to pay dividends is a retained earnings' test. If a company retains $1 in earnings, can it turn that into more than $1 in increased market value? If it can, shareholders should logically prefer reinvestment of earnings, and those seeking income may sell shares as needed.

If a company is not meeting the retained earnings' test, then I would argue it is destroying value by retaining earnings and therefore has an obligation to pay dividends so that shareholders may redirect their capital to more attractive rates of return.

This dynamic of dividends and stock price has a simple analogy. Think of your portfolio as a pair of pants. Let's say you own a stock and you keep that in your left pocket. If that stock pays a dividend, what's happening is value is moving from your left pocket and going into your right pocket. The total value and weight of what's in your pockets is the same. You're just shifting money around. Unfortunately, when the government sees your money move from one pocket to another, it taxes it.

What I've explained to you, I explained to Charlotte. It opened her eyes. She began to move her investments—not all at once, but in a better direction.

The next question for her—and for you, I hope—is where that opportunity lies.

IF YOU REMEMBER ONE THING...

If your stock pays one dollar in dividends, expect the price of the stock to go down by one dollar.

CHAPTER TWO

THE BETTER WAY

I NOTICED A TREND WHILE I WAS WORKING AT SCHWAB. I consistently heard management and executives speaking excitedly and adamantly about the future and all the wonderful growth opportunities that we had. At the same time, I also noticed that the company's quarterly dividend was consistently going up. This did not make sense to me. Why were we pushing so much money out of the company in the form of dividends when we could instead be investing more in new opportunities? I could not come up with a good answer. I began asking that question again: why?

I asked my manager and then our vice president. Then our senior vice president, and then our executive vice president. None had a great answer. Eventually, I had the chance to attend a presentation by a Schwab senior executive. After it concluded, I approached and put the question to him, one on one: "Why are we paying so much in dividends and continuing to increase them?"

"Well," he said, "between you and me, it's because Chuck wants income."

That was my aha moment. I finally understood the reason for the company's policy. Chuck Schwab owns 10 percent of the company he started, and he wants income from it. At the time, the dividends the company paid were bringing Chuck roughly $87 million every year. How about *that* for a retirement plan? I tried to put myself in his shoes and think things through. "Well, if I'm Chuck," I thought to myself, "what would I be doing differently to create a better outcome not only for myself but for the shareholders and the entire company?"

After thinking on this for a few weeks, I crafted a two-page letter addressed to Chuck. I had to get it approved by my senior vice president, and then I had to send it to Chuck's chief of staff, Greg Gable. About six weeks later, I got an email back from Greg. It read, "Chuck has read your letter and he's intrigued with your idea. He would like to meet with you in the San Francisco office." I scheduled the meeting and bought my plane ticket.

INCOME ON DEMAND

I'll tell you about what happened once I sat down with Chuck and his chief of staff later in this chapter. But first let me tell you about the case I made, because it's the case I make to my clients, and it's the case I'm making in this book. I think of it as "The Better Way."

The conventional way of getting income from stocks is through dividends. We've covered that already. The alternative strategy—what I think of as the better way—is to sell shares that have appreciated in price. You have the ability to do that with just about any individual stock or fund. All things being equal, I strongly prefer an index fund. An index fund will contain stocks that pay dividends because it represents the overall market, but the dividend stocks are only a small part of this larger mix. It's a growth-oriented investment that can offer a better total return than dividend-paying stocks alone. When you need income, you sell some of your shares. More specifically, you sell in proportion to how much your fund is appreciating in price. If it's not appreciating, you're not selling. If it's appreciating dramatically, you have the *option* to sell much more.

It may help to think of the two approaches as money trees.

Focusing on dividends is like owning an apple tree. An apple tree grows to maturity and then tends to slow its growth. But every year it produces apples that you can pick. That's your income. I think of AT&T as an apple tree; ExxonMobil as well. They tend to bear fruit every year. That strategy for income can work; I'm not arguing it's the *wrong* way. But I do believe there's a better way.

The alternative I prefer is to own a stock through an index fund that focuses on total return, a combination of price appreciation and some dividends. I think of that as owning an oak tree. Every year, for decades, an oak tree gets bigger and stronger, bigger and stronger. Amazon is an oak tree; so is Apple. Your oak tree is going to kick off acorns every year—perhaps a little bit in dividends. But for the most part, when you want income, you can simply trim from the new branches and foliage that your oak tree produces.

You take from growth—and avoid cutting into the trunk (the principal). If circumstances permit, you can allow it to keep growing and strengthening over time. Not only will that benefit you as the years pass; it can set up your beneficiaries to inherit something much more substantial than an apple tree. Oak trees cast more shade.

MORE GROWTH, LESS TAXES

The benefits of a growth-based approach begin, naturally enough, with growth. It just makes sense, if you stop and think about it. Dividend-paying companies, or dividend-driven mutual funds, often represent a more mature sector of the stock market that may not grow as fast as the market as a whole. By definition, the whole market represents the full mix of companies, driven forward by those that are growing the fastest, that see the most opportunity, and are doing the best to take advantage of it. With each passing year, as these companies produce profits, they reinvest the money, generating still more profits. Each year's growth builds on the next, which puts the power of compounding interest to work on your behalf.

"Well-managed industrial companies do not, as a rule, distribute to the shareholders the whole of their earned profits," wrote John Maynard Keynes, one of the foremost economists of the twentieth century. "In good years, if not in all years, they retain a part of their profits and put them back into the business. Thus there is an element of *compound interest* operating in favor of a sound industrial development." Keynes is not referring to reinvesting dividends—an activity that puts a tax liability on shareholders. He's referring to retained profits, money earned by the company and retained in the company—an activity that does not put any tax liability on shareholders.

The numbers support what strikes me as common sense. Consider the accompanying chart. If you had invested $100,000 in a low-cost S&P 500 ETF fund—an approximation of the overall market—in 2007, you'd have had nearly $296,000 by November of 2019. If you'd put the same sum in one of the three popular dividend-based funds, you'd have as much as $60,000 less. Remember, you're not losing out on dividends altogether when you invest in the overall market. The point is that an index fund has the potential to offer better total return—how much you receive in income plus price appreciation. The table below illustrates the returns of a low-cost S&P 500 index fund versus three popular dividend ETFs. Each column represents a fund, and the return figures below it represent the performance over a specific time period.

Performance of an S&P 500 Fund vs.
Three Popular Dividend Funds

Data for 13 years ending Nov. 30, 2019.

Fund Name	iShares Core S&P 500 ETF	SPDR® S&P Dividend ETF	Vanguard High Dividend Yield Index Fund ETF Shares	iShares Select Dividend ETF
Symbol	IVV	SDY	VYM	DVY
YTD	27.52%	20.89%	20.49%	19.38%
1 Month	3.64%	1.91%	2.34%	1.62%
3 Months	7.94%	7.64%	7.45%	6.91%
6 Months	15.25%	12.28%	12.99%	12.88%
1 Year	16.22%	11.48%	10.08%	9.86%
3 Year	14.86%	11.57%	10.76%	9.53%
5 Year	10.94%	10.30%	8.90%	9.18%
13 Year	8.7%	8.29%	7.93%	6.84%

You might be asking yourself, how does the S&P 500 compare to dividend funds when the market is down? The coronavirus pandemic brought a down-market that shows us. In the next chart, notice how the same S&P 500 and three popular dividend funds performed in the first three months of 2020. The dividend funds performed worse than the S&P 500.

Performance of an S&P 500 Fund vs.
Three Popular Dividend Funds During 2020 Bear Market

Data for the first three months of 2020

Fund Name	iShares Core S&P 500 ETF	SPDR® S&P Dividend ETF	Vanguard High Dividend Yield Index Fund ETF Shares	iShares Select Dividend ETF
Symbol	IVV	SDY	VYM	DVY
Performance	-19.56%	-25.08%	-23.97%	-29.46%

The second benefit of a growth-based approach is taxes, and it's considerable. Remember, dividend income is fully taxable if it's not in a retirement account. That's true even if you reinvest the dividend. You're reporting your dividends to the IRS every year, and you're being taxed on them as income. But—and I'd ask you to read carefully what's coming next because it's important—when you get income by selling shares, *the IRS will only tax you on the gain you've enjoyed since you bought in.*

For a more eloquent illustration of these benefits, we turn to the Oracle of Omaha.

WARREN BUFFETT'S EXAMPLE

I wrote earlier of the education I received—and the inspiration I took—from Warren Buffett's annual letters to Berkshire Hathaway shareholders. In 2012, his letter addressed the question of dividends head on. Why, some shareholders were asking, didn't Berkshire Hathaway pay dividends?

He laid out his reasoning through a hypothetical example. Imagine that you and I, he wrote, are equal owners of a business that's worth $2 million. And imagine that it can earn a 12 percent return—or $240,000—each year.

You want income and propose that each year our company invests two-thirds of those earnings in growth, while paying out a third of its earnings in dividends—a nice little check of $40,000 for each of us in the first year, growing over time as the value of the company continues to increase. Sounds good, right?

But then, Buffett asks, consider an alternative: reinvest all our company's earnings in growth and sell 3.2 percent of our shares each year. He called this a "sell-off" approach. The first year's check would be the same $40,000. But the company will grow a third faster with each passing year. Look out ten years, he argued; the result is an even bigger win-win. The value of your shares would be higher, and your annual payouts would be higher too. "Voila!" Buffett wrote. "You would have both more cash to spend *and* more capital value."

Below is a visualization of his example with a couple adjustments. For simplicity, it combines the two owners into one owner. And I added two assumptions: first, since the business has a net worth of $2 million, I assumed a cost basis of $2 million. Second, I assumed a tax rate of 20 percent. I assumed 20 percent because most dividends are recognized as 'qualified' dividends and fall under the tax schedule of long-term capital gains. Under that schedule, it's common for investors to pay a 15 percent federal tax rate plus their applicable state tax rate.

Notice two things in the following table: in the sell-off scenario, the owner ends up with 72 percent ownership in the company, but this fraction is still worth more than owning the entire "dividend company." You can view that comparison in the far-right column. Second, notice how income from selling shares is higher than income from dividends every year, and significantly higher when taxes are factored in.

DIVIDENDS SCENARIO

YEARS	COMPANY NET WORTH	COMPANY MARKET VALUE	PRE-TAX INCOME	AFTER-TAX INCOME	PERCENTAGE OWNERSHIP	VALUE OF OWNERSHIP INTEREST
1	$2,000,000	$2,500,000	$80,000	$64,000	100%	$2,500,000
2	$2,160,000	$2,700,000	$86,400	$69,120	100%	$2,700,000
3	$2,332,800	$2,916,000	$93,312	$74,650	100%	$2,916,000
4	$2,519,424	$3,149,280	$100,777	$80,622	100%	$3,149,280
5	$2,720,978	$3,401,222	$108,839	$87,071	100%	$3,401,222
6	$2,938,656	$3,673,320	$117,546	$94,037	100%	$3,673,320
7	$3,173,749	$3,967,186	$126,950	$101,560	100%	$3,967,186
8	$3,427,649	$4,284,561	$137,106	$109,685	100%	$4,284,561
9	$3,701,860	$4,627,326	$148,074	$118,460	100%	$4,627,326
10	$3,998,009	$4,997,512	$159,920	$127,936	100%	$4,997,512
11	$4,317,850	$5,397,312	$172,714	$138,171	100%	$5,397,312

SELL-OFF SCENARIO

YEARS	COMPANY NET WORTH	COMPANY MARKET VALUE	PRE-TAX INCOME	AFTER-TAX INCOME	PERCENTAGE OWNERSHIP	VALUE OF OWNERSHIP INTEREST
1	$2,000,000	$2,500,000	$80,000	$76,800	100%	$2,500,000
2	$2,240,000	$2,800,000	$86,733	$81,777	96.80%	$2,710,400
3	$2,508,800	$3,136,000	$94,032	$87,220	93.70%	$2,938,507
4	$2,809,856	$3,512,320	$101,946	$93,167	90.70%	$3,185,812
5	$3,147,039	$3,933,798	$110,526	$99,659	87.80%	$3,453,930
6	$3,524,683	$4,405,854	$119,828	$106,741	84.99%	$3,744,613
7	$3,947,645	$4,934,557	$129,912	$114,461	82.27%	$4,059,759
8	$4,421,363	$5,526,704	$140,846	$122,870	79.64%	$4,401,429
9	$4,951,926	$6,189,908	$152,699	$132,027	77.09%	$4,771,853
10	$5,546,158	$6,932,697	$165,550	$141,992	74.62%	$5,173,452
11	$6,211,696	$7,764,621	$179,483	$152,833	72.24%	$5,608,850

This scenario is used with permission from Warren Buffett.

In the dividend scenario over ten years, dividends produced pretax income of $1,158,925. After 20 percent taxes are applied, this leaves after-tax income of $927,140.

In the sell-off scenario over ten years, share sales produced pretax income of $1,182,072. After 20 percent taxes are applied to the gain portion of sales, this leaves after-tax income of $1,209,547.

The sell-off strategy not only produced an additional $23,147 of income, it saved a whopping $282,407 in taxes over ten years. What would you do with that kind of tax savings?

By using the sell-off strategy in this example, the owner's effective tax rate is nearly cut in half, from 20 percent to 10.6 percent! Moreover, the owner enjoys greater growth of principal and greater income.

In his 2012 letter, Buffett goes on to explain two further benefits of the selling strategy over the conventional dividend policy. First, more control; second, less tax. "The sell-off alternative," he wrote, "lets each shareholder make his own choice between cash receipts and capital build-up."

The second disadvantage of the dividend approach that Buffett described is of equal importance. "The tax consequences for all taxpaying shareholders are inferior—usually far inferior—to those under the sell-off program. Under the dividend program, all of the cash received by shareholders each year is taxed whereas the sell-off program results in tax on only the gain portion of the cash receipts."

Buffett quite rightly points out that the sell-off program results in tax on only the gain portion of the cash receipts. But what exactly does that mean? If you sell shares of stock that have doubled in price, only 50 percent of the cash you receive is taxable. From an accounting perspective, the IRS considers the other 50 percent to be part of your cost basis and therefore **tax-free!** This is a huge leap forward compared to dividends, which in a taxable account are always 100 percent taxable.

Buffett's lesson to Berkshire shareholders clearly worked. A few years ago, a Berkshire Hathaway shareholder put forward a proposal for a vote on paying a dividend. He allowed the vote to occur. The result was as close to a communist election tally as you can come in an actual, fair, straight-up vote: shareholders voted 98 percent in favor of no dividend.

CONTROL YOUR INCOME

Companies that pay dividends choose to cut them only rarely, in dire circumstances, because the market takes that as a sign of weakness and it can force institutional income investors to dump their stock. That's why dividend payments are so consistent. To return to my apple and oak tree analogy, dividends are the apples that tend to fall every season. But one downside of this dividend harvest is that you don't have a choice about when or how many apples fall your way. Whatever the company wants to do, that's what you're going to get.

The reality of retirement life is your needs and your spending change over time. Let's say you retire at age sixty-six. You decide to hold off on taking Social Security until you're seventy, because your payments will be 32 percent higher if you wait. That's great. But you need income. So, you start living on your portfolio.

When you hit seventy, suddenly you're taking your Social Security and your recurring cash flow jumps significantly. Now you may consider dialing back the income you're taking from your portfolio.

A dividend strategy can make that difficult; a sell-off strategy can make it easy.

For most people, income needs change as they age, too. Generally speaking, you will need significantly less income as you grow older. In 2016, a writer named David Blanchett laid out the findings of a University of Michigan study on retirement spending in an article in the *Wall Street Journal*. For every dollar retirees spent at age sixty-five, he wrote, they were only spending eighty cents twenty years later, even when you consider inflation. For people who are able to spend at a higher level early in retirement, the drop is even more substantial—from a dollar at age sixty-five to seventy cents at age eighty-five. Healthcare, he noted, can be the anomaly, but in general, spending slows down. Most people don't need their income to go up every single year, no matter what.

WHAT HISTORY TELLS US

We can't see what the future will bring—but we can learn from the past. One of my favorite websites is portfoliovisualizer. com. It provides a back-testing tool that lets you see how actual portfolios—and actual withdrawal rates—would have worked over any date range beginning as far back as 1985. I want to show you a purely hypothetical example for illustrative purposes only. If you retired then, at sixty-five, and utilized the income-on-demand strategy, where would you stand in 2019, at age ninety-nine? On the other side of a dot-com bust and the Great Recession?

We start with some assumptions. Let's say the beginning portfolio balance is $1 million, invested entirely in Vanguard's S&P 500 index fund. Let's say you want income worth 5 percent of the portfolio's value every year to help finance your hypothetical retirement.

The results are startling. Over those thirty-plus years, you'd have taken a total of $7,348,554 in income—and your ending portfolio balance would stand at $6,869,081. I'll let the numbers speak for themselves in these charts.

Annual Withdrawals

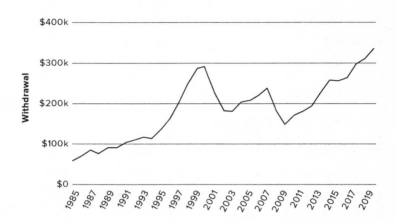

Portfolio Growth

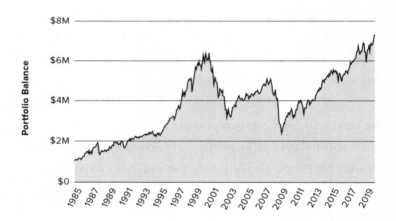

Of course, there's also the worst-case scenario. What if you happened to retire at the worst possible time in this period? That would be 1999, at the peak just before the dot-com bust, with the Great Recession still to come.

The numbers don't work as well, to be sure. But they still work—even if you withdraw 5 percent of your portfolio value. Your initial balance of $1 million would stand at $1.3 million—and you'd have taken $956,401 in income along the way.

MAKING THE CASE TO CHUCK

"Dear Mr. Schwab,

The progress of Schwab over the past four decades has been nothing short of phenomenal. I've read through the history of the company and found that after we went public, stockholders looked to balance the need for current income with capital growth. Since 1989 the dividend payout has been rising at a commensurate rate with earnings growth and the ending result has been wonderful. I want to acknowledge the need for stockholders to continue increasing their income from the business over time, but I wish to suggest that continuing to raise the quarterly dividend represents only the company's second-best option for achieving that end. I am writing because I want to share with you a strategy that allows yourself and all stockholders to increase income from the business in a more tax-advantageous way."

That's how I began my letter to Chuck Schwab, outlining the case for change at his company based on the principles I've described in this book. I went on to show Chuck how taking, say, an additional $5 million in income from selling shares rather than dividends would save him $333,000 a year in taxes. I described how all shareholders could benefit from adopting this sell-off approach. I argued that money invested in Schwab itself rather than paid out in dividends would accelerate the company's growth. And I was realistic. I didn't argue that we should stop paying dividends; instead, I said, we should simply stop increasing them.

"This move is not just in your best interest or the company's best interest," I closed. "Because of how well it capitalizes and sets Schwab up for continued growth and innovation, it's most importantly in the best interest of our clients."

The letter made an impact. I was invited to visit Chuck in his office to discuss it. I met him on the top floor of Schwab headquarters in San Francisco. He has the plushest carpet I've ever stood on, so thick and soft I felt like I was walking on a cloud. Greg Gable, his chief of staff, joined us. "Nice to meet you, JD," Chuck said as he shook my hand. "Why don't you come sit down and you can win me over on your proposal?"

At this point, Chuck was eighty-one years old. I was thirty. He had founded a company that pioneered discount stock sales back in 1975, and brought trading commissions to $0 by 2019. At the time we met, the company bearing his name employed fourteen thousand people and maintained ten million client accounts. His net worth stood above $8 billion.

Chuck was warm, welcoming, and curious about my background and my work with the company. Greg complimented the case I made, saying it would allow shareholders to take income on their terms, which aligned well with the company's core commitment to "serve clients on their terms." But when the conversation turned to my proposal, Chuck didn't ask me to expand on what I'd written or even to talk about it.

"JD, I agree with you that financially we would be better off if we did this," he said. "But there are important non-financial reasons why we're not going to do it." He told me that, as a financial services company, the market expected Schwab to pay a dividend. Paying dividends, he added, also helps Schwab broaden its investor base. A broader base, he said, helped protect the company from a takeover and the culture change that could come with it. And finally, he said this, "If we use this strategy, you're right, it's going to minimize the taxes that we pay, but we don't want to minimize our taxes too much."

At that point I realized he simply didn't want to change.

"Let me tell you why we started paying a dividend in the very first place," he said. "I needed income. I always insisted on taking a lower salary, so I needed income." There it was in a nutshell.

He was easy to like. He had a good sense of humor and

struck me as a genuinely nice guy. When I mentioned my background in golf, he looked at Greg. "Why aren't we on the golf course right now?" he joked.

"I love growth just as much as the next man," Chuck told me as I left. "If you have a growth idea, let me know. Contact me again and we'll play golf next time." That's what he said. What I heard was: at this stage in his successful life, he wasn't interested in changing his company's dividends' practice or the way he took his income.

The Charles Schwab Corporation has its reasons for maintaining its dividend policy. However, I left that meeting every bit as convinced that there was a better way for individuals like you to generate income. In the next chapter, I'll show you how to lay the foundation for it.

IF YOU REMEMBER ONE THING...

Dividend income is 100 percent taxable. Selling shares for income enjoys a tax advantage: only the gain portion is taxed—the rest is tax-free.

CHAPTER THREE

DEVELOPING
YOUR PLAN

THE MASTERS GOLF TOURNAMENT IS HELD EVERY
April amid the beautiful, blooming flowers in Augusta,
Georgia. It's one of the four major professional tourna-
ments ever year, and my personal favorite. As the 2007
Masters drew near, no one gave golfer Zach Johnson a
chance. He was ranked fifty-sixth in the world at the
time; only the top sixty scorers in the first two rounds
of the tournament even make the final two rounds, so
his ranking suggested he was much closer to missing the
cut than winning. The world's best golfer, Tiger Woods,
was in his prime, and the second-best golfer wasn't even
close to him. Augusta favored long hitters. Woods was
the longest, while Johnson was one of the shortest on the
tour. To say he was coming in under the radar would be
an understatement.

But Johnson won. I'd argue that he won even before he ever teed it up on the first hole. That's because Johnson created a plan that set him up for success in the unseasonably cold, wet weather that settled over Augusta the week of the 2007 tournament. That weather made the course play even longer than usual, so the odds on favorites like Woods who typically overpowered it with long drives lost their great advantage. The conditions also played right into Johnson's hands. He knew he couldn't overpower Augusta, no matter what the weather, so he decided to lay up on all the par fives and rely on his short game to get the job done. Augusta features four par fives, monstrously long holes, and Johnson laid up on every one of the sixteen times he played them. His score for the week on those holes was eleven under par, which is great even in normal conditions. That gave Johnson an edge that neither Woods nor any of the other top competitors could overcome. He won by two shots and took home the famous Green Jacket. He also took home the winner's purse of $1.3 million.

My point here is that if Zach Johnson can win the Masters only by creating and following a plan, you can succeed in retirement by creating and following a financial plan. The income-on-demand strategy that I've discussed is very powerful, but it is just a strategy. You need a roadmap to see if using the strategy is in your best interest, and if so, how to use that strategy effectively. A financial plan is that roadmap.

CREATING YOUR PLAN

A financial plan is by its very essence reducible to mathematical formulas, but it begins with a conversation. When I sit down with a client or a couple to prepare their plan, I begin by gathering as much information as I can on their current financial situation: what's their income from all sources, what are their expenses, both debt-related and non-debt-related, and what are their assets, whether it's real estate, a business, an investment portfolio, or cash in the bank.

That's where they are today. Next, in the course of conversation, I seek to understand where they want to be in the future. Maybe that's a certain spending goal and lifestyle. For some it's gifting to their kids or gifting to charity. It's all equally valid.

Only then do I run the numbers, carrying today's numbers and the client's aspirations out over the retirement years to come. The results will show, for example, what rate of return the clients need to meet their goals. It will show how soon they can retire, based on the lifestyle they want. It will tell them how much they can afford to spend, or how much they can afford to give away. And—here's an aspect of a financial plan that I really like—it can give the clients a good idea of what their asset balances or net worth might look like in ten or twenty years, so they know how much they could be leaving to heirs or other beneficiaries.

That's the beauty of a financial plan. It's an individualized "roadmap." You plug in any preferences you want. Maybe it's no highways, no toll roads, whatever it may be, and it's going to show you how to get to your destination the way that you want to get there.

A financial plan is not a cure-all. If you have unsustainable financial habits—say you're spending too much—a financial plan is not going to fix that right away. It will, however, show you what needs to change, and knowing that something needs to change is immensely valuable. The plan is there to show you what your options are.

A financial plan is a projection based on sound assumptions. It is realistic and as practical as we can make it. It will show you concrete steps that you can take in order to meet the goals that you have. Maybe that involves changing your portfolio or adjusting your budget in some fashion. Armed with a better understanding of your goals and how to get there, you might find you need some form of insurance that you don't currently have.

There's great value in the process of developing a financial plan too. I've found that many people haven't really thought through what they want to do in their retirement. I'll ask, "Okay, what do you want your retirement to look like?" And they'll answer, "Well, I'm not really sure." They know they don't want to work forever, but they haven't thought through specifically what their day-to-day life will look like or how they'll spend their day to day to enjoy their retirement. A financial plan gives you the opportunity to find these answers. In cases where one partner handles the finances, developing a plan together will ensure both understand the big picture and share a sense of priorities. If you're hands on, developing a plan provides an opportunity to refamiliarize yourself with your expenses and current situation. There's even value in documenting your accounts and account numbers and balances in one place at one time, because in the course of normal life, that may not happen.

One final benefit of developing a financial plan is that it can offer peace of mind and the confidence that goes with it. I've had clients who, for whatever reason, just felt they didn't have enough money for retirement. They thought that they couldn't go on that special family trip that they dreamed of because if they spent like that, they'd jeopardize their retirement. But if they're basing their decision on a plan that illustrates, even with a crummy market, that they're going to be just fine—well, all of a sudden, they have the peace of mind and comfort level that gets them on a plane and off on their adventure.

Let me illustrate both sides of the equation: unrealistic expectations on the one hand, and a lack of confidence on the other.

I recently prepared a financial plan for a couple from San Diego, California. They came to me with a wildly exaggerated sense of how well their portfolio was doing and what they could spend on an ongoing basis. I told them right off that I wanted to do a financial plan. The results of the plan surprised them.

"Folks," I said, "let's assume very optimistic scenarios with the market, and here's how much we could take out. Here's how much you're spending. There's this very wide gap between the two. The hard truth is you are on an unsustainable path right now. Go to any advisor you want, but no one's going to assume growth of 15 percent a year in the market and call that reliable."

To their credit, they listened and said, "Okay, well, we need to reevaluate our aggressive spending rate." They took what the plan showed seriously, found opportunities to reduce their spending, and made it sustainable. They corrected what was a disastrous trajectory.

I've seen a lack of confidence drive bad choices too. I've often found that when a client doesn't know how much they need to support their retirement, either their conscious or subconscious mind drives them toward trying to maximize every bit of return that they can possibly get. They think they've got to keep working as long as they can and chase every ounce of return, owning more stocks than they need to—and it's all because of the uncertainty in the back of their mind.

That dynamic reminds me of something I see again and again on golf tee boxes across the country. On standard par-four holes, professional golfers don't always use their driver. Instead, a pro will visualize the hole in reverse. They'll ask themselves, "What club am I comfortable hitting into the green?" That could be a 7-iron or an 8-iron. Knowing that they'll ask, "What club do I need to hit off the tee to set up that approach shot?" The answer is often 3-wood, a hybrid, or maybe a driving iron. They know that they don't need that max power for success. But an amateur golfer? They don't bother checking how long the hole is and there is no plan. They walk up on a par-four tee and pound away with driver. Call in the search and rescue team to find where the ball ended up.

GETTING PROFESSIONAL HELP

Someone who is unfamiliar with the complexities of retirement planning may find it difficult to develop a financial plan on their own. So, if you're not working with a planner already, how do you find one?

First of all, I recommend seeking out a Certified Financial Planner™. A planner who has earned that designation will put those initials after their name. It represents a level of training that has become the gold standard for the financial services industry today. It used to be that once you earned a Series 7 license as a broker or a Series 65 license as an advisor, you were considered to have a sufficient degree of expertise and aptitude to manage money for others. But the industry has evolved, and we've seen a shift toward an understanding that advisors today need to have a higher level of responsibility for their clients as well as an expertise that extends beyond a client's portfolio.

A stockbroker today is held to what's called a suitability standard. That means they are required by regulation to recommend only investments that are suitable for you in terms of your goals, risk tolerance, time horizon, and so on.

The higher standard that CFP® professionals must meet is called the fiduciary standard. It carries all of the requirements of the suitability standard and goes a step further by saying that they must also act in the client's best interest. They must put the client's interests first. With a suitability standard, for example, someone could recommend a high-commission product to you as long as it's "suitable." But is a high-commission product really in your best interest? With all the alternatives in today's environment, the answer is probably not. Fiduciaries have a responsibility to be diligent about keeping client fees low. To be fair, you can also find investment advisors who serve as a fiduciary and do not hold the CFP designation. These are still legitimate advisors. However, I strongly prefer advisors who are held to the fiduciary standard.

The second difference is expertise that extends beyond the client's portfolio. When someone goes through the CFP process, they gain aptitude in six areas: insurance, estate planning, investments, retirement planning, ethics, and tax planning. It's a holistic designation. When you talk with a CFP, you're talking with someone who can provide tools and resources in areas outside of your portfolio. Can brokers also provide value in those other areas? Yes, absolutely. Just know there is no standardized process for their gaining expertise in those areas.

WHERE TO LOOK?

The next question becomes, how do you find a CFP? And beyond that, what's an affordable price?

If you are looking to find an advisor locally, I would recommend the National Association of Personal Financial Advisors (NAPFA). You can Google it, or simply go to napfa. org. This is a large, nationwide network of advisors who are willing to create one-time financial plans for a fee (among other services as well) and have taken a fiduciary oath. You can begin by using the "Find an Advisor" tool on the home page.

Here's another option: If you happen to have an account

with Schwab already, the company provides a do-it-yourself option at no cost. Just search the site for the Retirement Savings Calculator, enter your information and you'll see where you stand. I've used this before and found it helpful, considering that it takes only ten minutes and is free. If you used another major brokerage firm, talk to your local contact to learn what planning options are available, and at what cost.

And, of course, there's also the old-fashioned way: word of mouth. Once you've got a name or names to consider, you'll need to do your homework, including learning what they'll charge.

The price can vary substantially. I would argue that spending $1,000 for a financial plan is worthwhile. It's going to shape your financial future. The value will far exceed that cost.

I think of it as analogous to going to the doctor for a full physical. "Okay," they'll say, "turns out you've got these health problems. We're going to put you on a better diet and prescribe this medication, and together we're going to significantly improve your quality of life." Would that kind of guidance be worth just a few hundred dollars to you, or a little bit more?

Once you've developed a plan, with or without an advisor,

you want to consider the type of investments that are right for you.

IF YOU REMEMBER ONE THING...

A financial plan answers the foundational question of retirement: How can I meet my financial goals in a way that works for me?

CHAPTER FOUR

MAKING THE RIGHT INVESTMENTS

IN DECEMBER OF 2007, WARREN BUFFETT PLACED A million-dollar wager with Protégé Partners, a hedge fund investment firm. It was a classic hare versus tortoise showdown. Buffett bet on the tortoise, wagering that the S&P 500 would outperform whatever five hedge funds Protégé Partners picked over a ten-year period. The winner would make a dramatic public point, and the money would go to charity.

Buffett acknowledged that Protégé Partners had the look of a winning hare. "This assembly is an elite crew loaded with brains, adrenaline, and confidence," he wrote. Still, Buffett believed that the tortoise—a virtually cost-free, unmanaged S&P 500 index fund—would win the race. And that was something Buffett wanted everyone with money in the stock market to know.

"Addressing this question is of enormous importance," he wrote to the shareholders in his company in 2017, at the conclusion of the race. "American investors pay staggering sums annually to advisors, often incurring several layers of consequential costs. In the aggregate, do these investors get their money's worth? Indeed, in the aggregate, do investors get *anything* for their outlays?"

The outcome of the race wasn't close: Buffett and his tortoise took the prize. In the first year, 2008, the hedge funds outperformed the index fund. Fast off the starting line! But in each of the next nine years, the index fund prevailed. Its annual average gain was 8.5 percent; the best of the five hedge funds checked in at 6.5 percent, and the worst at 0.3 percent.

By 2017, the money Buffett and Protégé Partners laid on the table had grown well beyond a million dollars. The beneficiary: Buffett's charity of choice, Girls Inc. of Omaha, with its $2.2 million windfall.

Buffett bet on the market itself, not on the ability of very smart people to pick a handful of winners from the crowd. What's more, hedge fund managers charge fees that are typically 2 percent of assets under management plus 20 percent of the annual performance. That tips the odds even further in favor of the index fund tortoise.

THE HARE: ACTIVE INVESTING

Generally speaking, there are two ways to approach investing in stocks. Active investing—the hare—is an attempt to outperform the overall stock market by purchasing stocks of individual companies, attempting to buy low and sell high. Passive investing means that you are simply owning the market, generally speaking by owning index funds. That's the tortoise.

I believe in the benefits of the tortoise. But in fairness, both have their pros and cons.

One pro of active investing is that you do have the potential to outperform the market—and in spectacular fashion. There are folks who invested in any one of Elon Musk's companies, from PayPal to Tesla or SpaceX. Given a sufficient time horizon, shareholders of these companies have both helped contribute to society in a positive way and made a ton of money in the process.

There are other examples. You could have bought Walmart stock on Dec. 14, 1979, at a split-adjusted fourteen cents a share; in late 2019, it was trading at $119.39. If you bought Apple in 1980 at a split-adjusted fifty-one cents a share, congratulations! The price stood at $266 in late 2019.

Still, it's critical to keep successes like these in perspective. They are few and far between. So are people who bought these stocks at the beginning, or who held on to them and simply rode the rocket up. Studies have documented what's called a behavior gap: the performance realized by actual investors has historically lagged the results delivered by the investments themselves—to the tune of 1.5 percent per year. Why? Investors are likely to buy in after stock prices run up, then sell when prices drop because they don't want to incur losses.

A second pro to active investing: it's very exciting to own individual companies, especially when their stock is appreciating and you're seeing positive narratives about those companies and their stocks in the news. Then you're telling your neighbor, "Hey, I bought Tesla stock a while back, and look at this amazing new car it's coming out with! It's going to have a full self-driving feature!" There's a tremendous positive reinforcement psychology behind this.

But there are cons, too.

For one thing, as Protégé Partners demonstrated, not every pick is a winner. And the very act of picking has its own cost. If you are doing it yourself, you are by definition spending a significant amount of time doing the research required to make stock picks that you believe will outperform. That's no easy task. That's a significant time commitment. If you're relying on an advisor who picks stocks, now you're going to have to spend time evaluating that manager to make sure that he's not underperforming too much and costing you money. What's more, when you tie yourself into the thrill of watching your stocks on the rise, you also tie yourself into the emotional downside too. The reality is, it's not always a thrill ride.

Here's another reality: according to Standard & Poor's, about 90 percent of active money managers have underperformed the S&P 500 over the past fifteen years. The one-year performance is slightly better—yet still 70 percent of professional managers underperform the market. I encourage you to see for yourself, as Standard & Poor's is constantly updating the numbers. You can find the latest figures by Googling "SPIVA statistics and reports." The following table shows what percentage of active funds tried to outperform the market and failed. The rows in this table refer to what size companies the active funds are investing in. Large Cap stands for Large Capitalization. This simply means large valuation—companies valued over $10 billion. Small Capitalization companies are valued at less than $2 billion. Mid-Cap are in between. Notice how the longer the time period gets, more funds tend to underperform.

Percentage of Active US Stock Funds
That Underperformed Their Benchmark

FUND CATEGORY	COMPARISON INDEX	1 YEAR	3 YEAR	5 YEAR	10 YEAR	15 YEAR
All Large-Cap Funds	S&P 500	64.49%	78.98%	82.14%	85.14%	91.62%
All Mid-Cap Funds	S&P MidCap 400	45.64%	74.29%	79.88%	88.03%	92.71%
All Small-Cap Funds	S&P SmallCap 600	68.45%	84.35%	89.40%	85.67%	96.73%

Data as of Dec. 31, 2018. Returns shown are annualized. Past performance is no guarantee of future results. Table is provided for illustrative purposes.

When clients of active managers question below-market performance, the answer they typically get—which is quite correct and truthful—is that they aren't fully invested in the market. Their portfolio is balanced with fixed-income investments. The manager might say, "We've put part of your portfolio into safe investments like bonds. Those safe investments have a lower return than the market. That's why your portfolio is underperforming the market." This is all true, but it avoids the point. It's important to take it one step further and examine how your stocks are doing against the overall market. In other words, how have the US stocks in your portfolio performed against the S&P 500? That's the apples-to-apples question. Ask it, and all your advisor can do is show you the numbers. Specifically, they will have to show you something called "asset-class performance." When you see the results, remember that anything can happen in the short term. I suggest looking at the three-year and five-year comparisons. If your investments in US stocks are lagging that S&P 500 benchmark over long time periods, you are losing money to opportunity cost—losing out on money you could otherwise have earned. Even if your stocks have appreciated in price and paid dividends but are lagging the benchmark, that active management is destroying portfolio value rather than adding it.

There are some exceptional active money managers out there. Unfortunately, their returns can still lag the market over a full market cycle.

One reason is the fees that active investments incur—typically 1 percent per year for an actively managed mutual fund. I've found many clients paying the standard 1 percent to their manager and paying another 1 percent to the active funds inside their portfolio. In the most insidious cases, multiple layers of fees can be stacked on top of each other, amounting to Russian doll of charges.

I once reviewed a client statement for an investor that held a "target-date retirement" mutual fund. In aggregate, there are tens of billions of dollars invested in these types of funds. You may hold one yourself. The idea is that the fund will provide an appropriate portfolio allocation for your time horizon so that you can set it and forget it. In this case, the target-date fund was a "fund of funds." In other words, the fund was made up of several other active mutual funds. They're not all structured this way, but in this instance, we found that the client was being charged *three levels of fees*. The first fee came from the funds inside the target fund, ranging from between 0.25 percent to 1 percent. Then the target fund itself charged its own fee of 1 percent, adding the second level. Then the advisor who recommended the fund to the client was charging his own fee of 1 percent. A total cost to client of at least 2.5 percent annually! This is the equivalent of a financial advisor calling in sick and invoicing you for the call.

Another downside of active investment: all the returns we've been discussing are pretax. Active management tends to lead to far more taxes than owning an index fund and going passive because of turnover.

By definition, an active manager is trying to identify a company that is selling for less than its intrinsic business value, and then hoping to sell it after it has appreciated to a fair valuation—to what it's really worth from a business perspective. Every time you do that, you sell at a gain, and you're going to pay tax. That means the best possible outcome for an active investor is to identify a few companies that are going to grow like gangbusters for a long time. Then you get the great returns and don't have to pay taxes due to turnover. Does it ever really play out that way? Very, very seldom. You don't hit on an early Amazon win very often.

The tax disadvantage applies to both individual stocks and an actively managed mutual fund. Such mutual funds pay out what's called a capital gain distribution almost every December, based on their calculation of your share of the gain they realized in turning over the stocks they hold. That doesn't add to the return on your investment, but it does add to your tax liability. If you're in such a fund, the figure to look for is its tax-cost ratio. According to the research firm Morningstar, the ratio typically runs between 1 and 1.2 percent. That means every year, you're going to lose one or two percentage points of performance because of the tax you're paying. Take a look at the mutual funds in your own brokerage account. What kind of tax-cost ratio are you paying?

One book I'd recommend is called *The Little Book of Common Sense Investing: The Only Way to Guarantee Your Fair Share of Stock Market Returns*. It's written by Jack Bogle, who founded Vanguard. Bogle lays out the full case for choosing passive index funds over active mutual funds or active managers. Along the way he quotes David Swensen, the chief investment officer of the Yale endowment fund, who sums up active investing nicely: "A minuscule 4 percent of funds produce market-beating after-tax results with a scant 0.6 percent annual margin of outperformance," or margin of gain, Swensen said. He continued: "The 96 percent of funds that failed to meet or beat the S&P 500 lose by a wealth-destroying margin of 4.8 percent per year."

That comes down to heads, you win a little bit; tails, you really lose. You have the potential to do better—paradoxically, by doing less.

THE TORTOISE: PASSIVE INVESTING

I worked at Schwab for about six years. Over that time, through my work responsibilities, I was able to view tens of thousands of accounts. I made it a habit, just out of personal curiosity, to view the portfolio performance of virtually everyone I spoke to. It was *extraordinarily* rare for me to find someone whose individual account performance was as good as an index fund, let alone better. And yet there were only a handful of occasions—perhaps five—when I came across someone who had simply decided to invest in an index fund. I remember asking one of them why he picked that strategy.

"Well, I actually lost so much money picking my own individual stocks," he said, "I just gave it up and thought, 'If you can't beat the indexes, join 'em.'"

Lesson well learned!

Some index funds, such as Vanguard's Total Stock Market fund, come as close as they can to owning every American stock out there. Others own a broad sample—such as Vanguard's S&P 500 fund, which represents 500 of America's largest and most profitable companies.

An active manager who strives to significantly outperform will often concentrate their bets. They might own ten stocks as their entire portfolio. You could argue that's sufficient diversification, but with an index fund the diversification question is put to bed. The very nature of a broad index fund ensures sufficient diversification. You essentially own the whole market.

A small fraction of that you'll give back in fees—but it's nothing like the 1 percent of assets an active fund typically charges. A prominent S&P 500 index fund today may charge an expense ratio of 0.02 percent to 0.05 percent. That amounts to fifty cents in fees for every $1,000 invested.

These fees are so low because an index fund is by its nature a commodity. There's no real differentiator between S&P 500 index funds offered by companies like BlackRock or Vanguard. The only way they can compete is by price, so they're going lower and lower and lower. In fact, as I write this book, Fidelity offers two funds that have an expense ratio of *zero*. It's actually conceivable to me that at some point, they'll be paying clients to invest in their index funds.

Index funds have a tax advantage, too. By its very nature, an index fund has little turnover. It's rare for companies within an index fund to be replaced. That means it's possible to own the same index fund for decades and avoid paying any capital gains tax until you actually sell shares.

You do give something up when you bet on the tortoise.

First, you have no potential for outperforming the market. You will never be able to tell your neighbor about that sexy individual stock that you bought just before it jumped ten times in value. I've had a couple clients raise that objection with me. I'll answer, "Why do you feel like your retirement portfolio should be exciting? Shouldn't getting the benefits you need be more important than it being exciting?"

When I spoke with Chuck Schwab that day in his office, our conversation turned to active versus passive management. "You and I both know that 99 percent of investors should be in an index fund because they're better off with that," he said. "The problem with index funds is they can be boring."

But does that matter? Let me share a quick analogy to illustrate how I view this topic. Every year, my father, some friends, and I hike the Grand Canyon from rim to rim. It's a stunning place and the hike has its hazards, but if you sufficiently train and prepare, it's an amazing experience.

Not everyone who sets out to hike the Grand Canyon has either trained *or* prepared. There's actually a book called *Over the Edge: Death in the Canyon* that describes all of the folly people have undertaken to get themselves killed while hiking there. I call it a catalog of inanities. People run down the trail and get exhausted, wander off the trail and get lost, or lean out over the edge and fall.

The job is to hike down, enjoy the views and some peace of mind, and then hike back up. That process can easily take over ten hours of hiking to complete. So, some people get all kinds of crazy ideas about how do it faster, to push the limits, or make it more thrilling. It reminds me of a lot of the active investing I've seen over the years.

In contrast there's a pack of mules that carry supplies and sightseers from the rim of the canyon to the base and up to the rim again. Now, a mule is a dumb animal—but you put a mule on a mission and you know what it does? *It acknowledges its limitations and ceases to be dumb.* How many times do you think a mule got itself killed because it tried to pee off the edge of the canyon to impress its friends? The answer is zero. Mules don't try to make their hike exciting. They just get the job done. Does it look boring? Yes, it can. Does it work? Yes. That to me is passive investing.

I will confess that I was once one of those risk-takers—not on the Grand Canyon hike, mind you, but in my personal investment strategy. When I started my own portfolio, I was an active investor. I was young, and I felt the thrill. But I didn't get results. After five years, I looked at my investments and found that I had not outperformed the S&P 500 by one iota. So, I said, "It's time to stop this." Today at least 90 percent of my net worth resides in index funds. I'm a reformed investor.

I'm not the only one. More and more investors are recognizing the advantages of passive management. At the end of August 2019, US index funds held $4.27 trillion in assets, according to Morningstar—a figure that, for the first time, surpassed the total held in actively managed funds, at $4.25 trillion. *The Wall Street Journal* described the moment as "the passing of the asset crown."

IF YOU REMEMBER ONE THING...

An S&P 500 index fund represents a slice of corporate America. Ownership in an index fund can help align your returns with American business, which has a historical record that can't be beat. It can also help to minimize both your costs and taxes.

CHAPTER FIVE

DISINHERITING THE IRS

DR. THOMAS, A SUCCESSFUL PLASTIC SURGEON IN Newport Beach, California, came to me seeking help with his financial planning and his portfolio. Like many investors, he had an IRA account, sheltered from taxation, and a taxable brokerage account too. It's a common setup. And, like many other clients I've worked with, this plastic surgeon had his assets in all the wrong places.

Sitting in his taxable account was a high-yield bond fund that was yielding about 5.5 percent. As a plastic surgeon in California, his income taxes were substantial. And bond interest is taxed as ordinary income—so he was losing half of his gain right off the top.

I presented him with a proposal for fixing that, along with

other changes in his portfolio. "There's this principle that we utilize called asset location," I explained, "and this just means that we need to put investments that generate a lot of tax inside of your IRA and investments that don't generate much tax inside your brokerage accounts."

My advice: sell the bond fund in your taxable account, then buy it back in your IRA. Overnight that saved him about $4,000 a year in taxes.

"Oh," he said, "I guess I didn't think about that."

Dr. Thomas was a very successful man. But I've learned that there are a lot of successful people who've earned a lot of money—and don't necessarily know anything about money management. That's not where their expertise lies. And that's okay! Recognizing what you don't know and choosing to delegate is perfectly rational.

The investment the doctor had chosen was outstanding. But where he put it was wrong. The lesson in his example is straightforward: Where you put your assets can save you a significant amount of money in taxes.

I'm not advocating tax evasion here. I believe everyone should pay their fair share of taxes. What I am advocating is tax avoidance—not paying more taxes than you have to—and that's both perfectly legal and entirely sensible.

ASSET LOCATION

First let me define my terms. An Individual Retirement Arrangement, most familiar as an IRA, is a tax-advantaged retirement account. A 401(k) is another type of tax-advantaged retirement account that is set up through your employer. By putting a portion of your paycheck into a pretax 401(k), you reduce your taxable income and may be eligible for a match from your employer. This allows you to defer paying taxes on your contributions and profits until you begin taking withdrawals. When the time comes, you'll pay those taxes at your ordinary income rate.

A Roth IRA is another type of retirement account. Cash you put into a Roth IRA comes from income that has already been taxed. Once it's inside the account, any profits you make are tax-free. If you hold your Roth IRA for a minimum of five years and wait till you are 59.5 years old, you can withdraw as much of the account as you like tax-free. Additionally, your contributions can be withdrawn tax-free at any time.

It's also likely that you have assets you couldn't contribute into an IRA, and those are in your brokerage account that's taxable. They could be stocks you inherited, among a multitude of other possibilities. Most clients who come to me have both account types, IRA and brokerage.

The old saying about the two things in life that are inevitable—death and taxes—is spot on. The IRS is going to hit you with its tax stick, and you can't avoid it. What you can influence is when it hits you, and how hard. That's a matter of where your assets are located and how they're invested.

I've laid out how different assets are taxed in the following chart. As you can see, any interest that you're earning, whether it's on cash, bond funds, individual bonds—that's going to be taxed as ordinary income. Dividends are taxed as income too; we've covered that. We've covered capital gains too; your tax rate depends on how long you've held your asset. For most people, the rate on a long-term capital gain is 15 percent. Any gains on collectibles, such as gold coins, have their own rate, 28 percent, but this often flies under the radar.

ASSET TYPES AND TAX CATEGORY

Cash Interest	Ordinary income
US Treasury bond interest	Ordinary income for Federal taxes. State tax-free
US Corporate bond interest	Ordinary income
State Municipal bonds	Federally tax-free. Also state tax-free if buying muni's in your state of resident
Preferred Stock dividends	Ordinary income if nonqualified, long-term capital gains if qualified
Real Estate Investment Trust (REIT) dividends	Ordinary income (with rare exceptions)
Common Stocks dividends	Ordinary income if nonqualified, long-term capital gains if qualified
Capital gain on stock sold within 365 days or less	Ordinary income
Capital gain on stock sold after at least one year and one day	Long-term capital gains
Collectibles	Ordinary income if less than one year, 28 percent if over one year

For clients who are still saving toward retirement, I'll discuss where it makes sense to locate their savings as they go forward. But most clients who come to me are well down the path toward retirement, and their flexibility in determining what goes where is more limited. For them, the question is: "What can we do with what we've already got?"

The most useful principle I can offer is this:

You can potentially minimize your tax bill by putting investments that will generate lots of tax inside your retirement accounts, while putting investments that won't generate much tax inside your brokerage account.

That's asset location. Your choices, of course, are influenced by your circumstances. There is no one-size-fits-all here. But, as the case of Dr. Thomas shows, applying that principle can save you thousands of dollars in taxes every year.

What would this mean in practice? Here are a few examples. Real Estate Investment Trusts, or REITs, are a popular investment because they yield a nice, juicy dividend. Income seekers tend to love REIT funds, but if you buy that in your brokerage account, your dividends are going to get taxed at ordinary income rates, which are the highest possible.

If you insist on holding individual stocks that you would sell based on their price, you may find you can save taxes putting these inside your IRA. The same applies for active stock mutual funds, which usually distribute capital gains every year because of the turnover within them that I discussed in chapter four.

On the other hand, there's a benefit to having investments that don't generate much tax in your brokerage or taxable account. This would include index funds. It would also include what I would call "forever stocks." This is somewhat common: people hold a stock that, for whatever reason, they never plan to sell. Maybe they inherit it from a parent who has passed; maybe their son or daughter works at the company; maybe they've just made a lot of money on it and they don't ever want to sell it. It can make sense to hold that type of asset in your brokerage account because if you never sell, you'll never pay the capital gains tax.

The graphic below illustrates the effect of various turnover rates on the value of your taxable account. It also compares this to holding stocks in your IRA. Assuming the same rate of return for each, zero percent turnover in the brokerage account produces the best result. Once we get to 10 percent turnover—meaning the stocks in your portfolio change every ten years—it produces a worse result than holding it in the IRA.

30-Year Wealth - Stock in IRA vs. Taxable Account at Various Turnover Rates

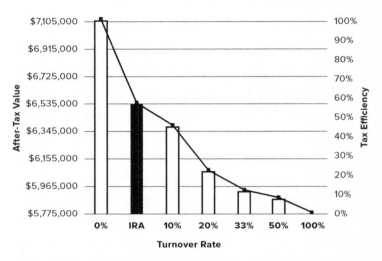

Credit to Michael Kitces and his blog Nerd's Eye View: https://www.kitces.com/blog/asset-location-for-stocks-in-a-brokerage-account-versus-ira-depends-on-time-horizon/

Now, these are principles—what you could think of as an all-options-open scenario. You may be in a position where you can't undo past choices. Even so, you can apply these principles to any choices you make going forward.

GIFTING TO HEIRS

Asset location isn't just about you and your retirement. It has significant consequences for your estate and what you leave your heirs. When you pass away, any investment sitting in your taxable account that has appreciated in value, however substantially, gets a really nice boost from the government. The cost basis on your investments get stepped up from the price on the date at which you acquired the asset to the date of your passing (or six months after). The gain that is embedded in that asset is erased, for tax purposes, and your heirs can sell it tax-free. One exception to this occurs for high-net-worth families who may face estate taxes.

When it comes to getting the benefits of cost basis step up, consider whether you are in a Community Property state (such as California, Arizona, or Texas) or a Common Law state, because there are differences between the two. Residents of the nine Community Property states may be able to get an extra benefit from cost basis step ups. Consult your tax professional or estate attorney for advice.

If that asset happens to be a forever stock or an index fund that has some significant appreciation behind it, you could die with several million dollars of unrealized gains—and all of a sudden your children can use it, no taxes owed.

There's a corollary to this benefit. It can actually be disadvantageous to concentrate your stock holdings inside an IRA that's meant to go to your kids after your passing. With the passing of the SECURE Act, the government mandates that the next-generation heir withdraws all assets inside that account within ten years. That also means they have to pay tax on every dollar of the account. There are some exceptions to this, but for a high-earning beneficiary, the value they receive could end up being dramatically less than the value at your passing.

What the government is trying to avoid with this rule is a generational tax dodge. Let's say I put money into my pretax IRA and avoid taxes on the gain in the value of that asset my whole life. I die. It passes to my kid. My kid avoids taxes on it his whole life, passes it on to his kid, and the cycle continues. To prevent that possibility, the government requires minimum distributions—minimum withdrawals, in essence, beginning when I turn 72, and if I pass along what's left to my kids, the government imposes Required Minimum Distributions, or RMDs, on them as well.

A Roth IRA is different, as we're about to see.

WITHDRAWAL ORDER

I have another client named John, a retired Boeing engineer in his mid-sixties who also lives in California. He also has a brokerage account and an IRA. He wasn't yet at the age where he was required to take a minimum distribution out of his IRA every year. John was living what I'd call a lavish lifestyle, and he was taking six-figure distributions out of his IRA to fund it—distributions taxable as ordinary income. This approach also pushed him into the highest Medicare premium bracket.

"Why are you doing it that way?" I asked.

"I didn't know it mattered."

It wasn't the first time I had heard something like this. Clients who come to me with both a brokerage account and an IRA often aren't as mindful as they could be about the consequences of how they take money out. But it does matter, to the tune of thousands of dollars in taxes every year.

I explained an alternative to John: Balance the fully taxable IRA distributions with sales from your brokerage account, where sales are partly tax free and your gains are taxed at the lower rates of long-term capital gains. The tax savings and Medicare premium savings amounted to well over 1 percent of his portfolio value every year.

That's the power of withdrawal order. It's important when you're living out your retirement, and it's important to the estate you leave behind as well.

Again, what I'm outlining here isn't a one-size-fits-all formula. Your goals for retirement and in estate planning will influence your choices. But for a client who wants to minimize their lifetime tax bill, the general principle for withdrawal order is this:

Spreading out your lifetime tax bill, by taking small and

voluntary tax hits earlier, can be more efficient than waiting and taking big, mandatory tax hits later.

Why is this the case? For two reasons.

First, the US tax system is progressive. The first dollars we earn in a year are taxed at a low rate, 10 percent. As we earn more, those additional dollars of income are taxed at increasing rates, up to 37 percent on the federal level. That means it's far better to take, say, $250,000 in income over two years than one. Take it in one year, and you'll pay a total of $62,693 in federal taxes. Take it over two years, and you'll pay a total of $48,348—a tax savings of $14,345 (based on a single filer in 2019).

The second reason goes back to those Required Minimum Distributions, which apply to traditional IRAs and 401(k)s. Starting at 72, you are required to withdrawal a certain percentage of your account every year as determined by an IRS calculation of life expectancy. As you get older, this percentage rises. If you were to live to 100, you could be required to withdraw 15.8 percent of your holdings in one year. For families with high net worth in particular, these required distributions can have a profound and pernicious effect. If you were to hold a $3 million IRA account at age 100, the government will require you to withdraw income of $474,000 and pay all the taxes that come with it.

If this concept seems tough to visualize, consider this analogy: Think of income as dry wood blocks. Think of taxes as fire. A large traditional IRA amounts to a giant stack of wood blocks. You can choose to make a slow-burning campfire that burns quietly ever year. Or you can hoard your wood blocks as long as possible—but only until the IRS requires you to build a bonfire.

That's why you may find yourself wanting to take full advantage of the progressive tax code, and avoid large mandatory taxes later in life. The question is how to do that.

Let me start by telling you what the answer usually is not: Depleting one account type entirely, then another, then another. If your advisor is telling you to follow the conventional wisdom of depleting your brokerage account, then your traditional IRA or 401(k), then your Roth IRA assets, I urge you to ask him or her to *quantify* their reason why. Ask them to show you the numbers that demonstrate why this works best. If you are your managing your own finances, I challenge you to write out your withdrawal strategy and detail the math behind your decisions. The exercise might change your thinking.

Experience and a lot of reading has led me in a different direction. I have found the best answer to be a blend of withdrawals from different account types, taking careful advantage of the annual lower marginal income brackets, and optimizing for a given client's individual financial goals.

CIRCUMSTANCES WILL VARY

What I've outlined won't make sense for everyone. If one of your goals is to maximize what your kids inherit, there will be other factors to consider. Let's say you're in your late eighties, and nearing the "end of retirement," and that you've got kids in their fifties with high-paying jobs. They're in the peak of their careers and already pay significantly higher tax rates than you because they're making more money. From their perspective, inheriting Roth assets will be significantly more beneficial than inheriting a pretax IRA. When they take that money out as part of their inheritance, they get it tax-free rather than adding to their tax bill (as long as the five-year rule has been met).

I've advised clients in this situation, especially if they're older and their income needs are lower, to convert some of their pretax assets into Roth assets and pay the tax bill—at a lower rate than their kids would—in doing it. Roth conversions can be a very useful legacy and estate-planning vehicle. It's most useful, in my experience, for clients who are in the range of age sixty-five to seventy. That's usually a window in which their income has dropped off. They're potentially not taking Social Security yet, having deferred so their payments, when they do take them, will be larger. That's a prime time for Roth conversions.

On the other hand, I've had clients, very nice people, whose kids are grown and successful, whose retirement philosophy amounts to this: "As a couple, our goal is to die with no money." There's nothing wrong with that. You've done your bit for your kids and it's your retirement to enjoy. Do not worry about Roth conversions. They probably shouldn't be a factor in your thinking.

MEASURES OF WHAT MATTERS

Wise asset location and well-tailored withdrawal order guidance are among the most valuable services a financial advisor provides. That's not just my opinion. Vanguard has made a study of the value their advisors provide to clients, quantified in basis points. (One basis point is equal to 1/100th of 1 percent.) Withdrawal order has potential value of up to 110 basis points and asset location, up to seventy-five. Add those two things together, and we're talking about a potential effect of 1.85 percent per year in an average client's net return. Grab a calculator. What's your current portfolio valued multiplied by 1.85 percent? This is a difference-maker.

Over time, that impact continues to add up. This is a case where I'm going to let numbers speak for themselves.

Below you'll find two charts generated using software from IncomeSolver® that calculates the effect of asset location and withdrawal order over time. The first illustrates the difference in the required minimum distributions you'd have to take if you left your traditional IRA to grow untouched versus what you'd face if you made partial Roth conversions to fill the 12 percent tax bracket earlier in your retirement. Remember, in the first case, those big distributions would come later in life, potentially pushing you into higher tax brackets, all at a time when your income needs might well be lower. Here are the assumptions behind the charts:

- Married couple in California retired by age sixty with a life expectancy of ninety
- Two-million-dollar portfolio—half in a Traditional IRA and half in a taxable account
- Portfolio is comprised of 70 percent stocks and 30 percent bonds
- Social Security payments begin at age seventy
- The conventional scenario holds the bulk of their stocks in an IRA, while the Roth scenario holds the bulk of their stocks in a brokerage account

Required Minimum Distributions

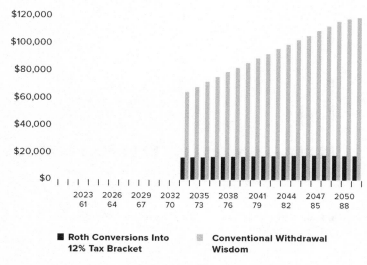

■ Roth Conversions Into
  12% Tax Bracket

░ Conventional Withdrawal
  Wisdom

Source: IncomeSolver® powered by Retiree, Inc., www.incomesolver.com

The second illustrates the difference in taxes you'd pay
under those two scenarios. Yes, it's painful to pay taxes
up front—but look at the potential savings in the long run.

Total Taxes

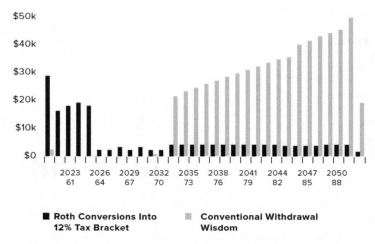

■ Roth Conversions Into
   12% Tax Bracket

▨ Conventional Withdrawal
   Wisdom

Source: IncomeSolver® powered by Retiree, Inc., www.incomesolver.com

The longer you expect to live, the more potential you have for Roth conversions to save you in taxes. Not everyone will benefit from Roth conversions. Talk to your advisor or tax professional about whether they could make sense for you.

IF YOU REMEMBER ONE THING...

Together, asset location and portfolio withdrawal order can influence your portfolio value by as much as 1.85 percent per year.

CHAPTER SIX

TRIMMING YOUR GROWTH TREE

LET ME INTRODUCE YOU TO ANOTHER CLIENT, PAT, who was about sixty-five when we met. He signed on with me in his first year of retirement. His portfolio was packed with good stocks: Google, Amazon, Salesforce, Netflix, Tesla, and more. Heavy hitters. Growth rockets.

"I've been doing some reading," he told me, "and I was wondering, should we go ahead and sell all of these non-dividend stocks that I have, and replace them with dividend-paying stocks so that we can generate income?"

That's when my hair started falling out.

Here's what Pat was thinking: These stocks don't pay dividends, so that means they don't produce income.

I'm a new retiree and I need income, so I need to switch to an investment that's better suited to my situation. These stocks helped me build wealth, and they built my nest egg. Now it's time to move on to income-producing assets.

Here's what I told him—and it should come as no surprise to you by now: The investments that fueled the growth in your portfolio can be the same ones you harvest for income in retirement. Yes, they are engines for wealth accumulation; shift your thinking, and you'll see they can work just as well for income production too. I showed him how much he'd pay in taxes if he sold all his existing stocks at once. And I laid out the downside of dividends: a stream of income you can't control, and more taxes than you need to pay. A lot more, every year.

THE CASE FOR GROWTH

The case I made to Pat for shifting to a growth-based income strategy is built on a core assumption: the overall market, as captured in the S&P 500, will continue to grow. Not every year—we'll discuss how to manage that reality in upcoming chapters—but over time. I understand why some might question this assumption. Headline news tends to carry a tone of uncertainty and fear. One side of the political aisle always worries the other side is about to destroy the country.

But the historical record only points in one direction. An investment made fifty years ago in the S&P 500, assuming reinvested dividends, has returned about 10 percent a year. As track records go, it's ridiculously good.

That's the past, some will say. What about the future?

It is a fair question. My personal expectation for American business is 7 percent returns per year over time. That's 5 percent from growth and 2 percent growth from dividends. Could that be wrong? Yes of course. The usual disclaimer applies. Past performance is not a guarantee of future results. But I'm not pulling that figure out of a hat.

The largest manager of assets in the world is a firm named BlackRock, with $7.4 trillion in client assets. On the Black-Rock website, you can read its expectations for all types of investments going forward in five-year intervals as far out as twenty-five years. Its take on US Large Cap equities—highly valued companies, such as those that make up the S&P 500—rises and falls over each of those intervals, but only by a little. Over the longest window, twenty-five years, BlackRock's expectation for US Large Cap growth is 7.4 percent a year.

You might ask why the market grows at all. It's because of the persistent and remarkable strength of the American economy.

In his *Little Book of Common Sense Investing*, Vanguard founder, Jack Bogle, lays out the growth in corporate profitability, beginning in 1900 and continuing over the twentieth century. It shows that, on average, every dollar of corporate investment yielded an average return of 9.5 percent over that time. And the market rose right along with it, at an average annual growth rate of 9.6 percent.

It's striking. The two figures are a literal match, marching up together over the decades. Over any extended period, the market tends to grow by the same rate as corporate profitability. "The miracle of compounding growth is a little short of amazing," Bogle wrote. "It is perhaps the ultimate winner's game."

HOW TO TRIM YOUR TREE

It's possible to implement an income-on-demand strategy on your own. To do that, you must know what steps to take and in what order. I'll lay them out for you here in summary form first.

STEP BY STEP

1. Identify the index fund or other equity investment of your choice and make your investment.

2. If it's in a taxable account, consider waiting 366 days to ensure you receive long-term capital gains tax treatment. This does not apply to retirement accounts.

3. Decide how often you're going to sell to generate income.

4. Determine how much income you need from the investment you've chosen.

5. Divide the dollar income you need by your principal amount. This shows your income requirement as a percentage of your investment.

6. If your investment pays a dividend, subtract your investment's dividend yield from the figure found in step 5. This updated figure represents the percentage of your investment that needs to be sold annually for income, net of the dividend.

7. Implement sales at your scheduled intervals. There you have it—income on demand!

Now let's cover each of those steps in more depth.

MAKE YOUR INVESTMENT

Your first step is investing the money you intend from which you'll take income as your portfolio grows. The choice is yours, of course, but if you wish to use an index fund, you can start by using your brokerage firm's "Fund

Screener" on their website. Major brokerage firms will have a research tool you can use to look for funds that meet your criteria, such as low cost and broadly diversified. You can also call your firm and ask for help identifying a fund.

In my view, it's critical to select a fund with a low net expense ratio. If you haven't heard of that term, it's worth reading what's next because it can affect your investments every year. The net expense ratio describes the fees that you're charged for owning a fund. It's expressed as a percentage of your investment in the fund. At any major brokerage firm, you'll find index funds with expense ratios at or below five basis points, or 0.05 percent of your investment.

If you can't identify those funds online on your own, my advice is simple: call your brokerage firm. They will point you in the right direction in less than sixty seconds.

Consider Picking an ETF to Save on Taxes

As I've mentioned, an index is simply a list of companies like the Dow Jones or S&P 500. An index fund is a product that tracks that list. It can take the form of either an ETF or a mutual fund. I will briefly explain their similarities and differences.

Same: Both an ETF and a mutual fund are a kind of basket that can hold stocks or bonds. Both an ETF and a mutual fund have a net expense ratio, which amounts to an ongoing cost of ownership.

Different: An ETF trades like a stock. A mutual fund trades once per day after the market has closed.

When picking index funds for a taxable account, as opposed to a retirement account, it is usually more tax advantageous to choose an ETF instead of a mutual fund.

The reason for this is because mutual fund capital gain distributions can cause you to pay taxes on the decisions other people make. Why? Because when an investor sells shares in a mutual fund, the fund has to sell the underlying shares of company stock that were inside your mutual fund shares. If the market has gone up, the fund recognizes a capital gain on the sale. After the mutual fund has sold the share, it distributes the cash to your account. But the tax that's due isn't paid only by you.

The mutual fund itself is just a big pool of money. Every investor in the fund is in the same pool. You might be a long-term investor who doesn't sell your mutual fund shares. But as other people sell shares, the mutual fund sells the underlying stocks inside them to generate the cash it needs to pay out. Whether you're selling shares or not, you're all in the same pool with everyone else—and so you owe your share of the taxes generated by other investors in the pool. The mutual fund will distribute the capital gains it generates to all its shareholders at the end of the year. This capital gain distribution will be paid out as cash and, like a dividend, will reduce the price of your fund.

ETFs are structured differently. When you buy or sell an ETF share, you're not selling the underlying companies inside the share. You're simply trading the share itself with another buyer or seller on the stock exchange. Because the ETF doesn't have to sell the underlying stocks, there are generally no capital gains generated to be distributed among all the shareholders. As a seller, you're only responsible for the capital gains generated by your own sale.

Whether you're looking to use the income-on-demand strategy with your own individual stocks or an index fund, be aware of your total expenses and try to keep them low. Make sure the size of your stock investment is aligned with the needs and solutions identified in your financial plan.

WAIT!

If you make an investment and sell it for a gain in less than one year, your gain is likely to be taxed at ordinary income rates. By waiting over one year, the IRS will grant you long-term capital gains treatment, which can significantly lower your taxes. The income-on-demand strategy will work significantly better if you sell from an investment held longer than one year.

PICK YOUR FREQUENCY

Next, you're going to choose how often you want to sell shares and generate income every year—in essence, generate your own dividend. It could be only once a year. It could be four times a year. At Farnam Financial, we do it twice a year. This is a preference, not a question of right or wrong.

DETERMINE HOW MUCH

Having chosen how often, next you determine how much. Your financial plan is your map to how much income you need each year, although of course you'll need to account for one-off expenditures—trip to Europe!—you've planned for the year to come. From that total, subtract the amount you're getting from any fixed-income investments in your portfolio, a pension, Social Security, and any other sources.

CONVERT TO A PERCENTAGE

What you're left with is the dollar amount you need from the stock side of the portfolio, your index fund. You'll divide that amount by the value of your stock holdings; that gives you the income percentage you need from that asset. For the sake of an example, let's call it 4 percent of the whole.

This is where most people would say, "Oh, okay, if my answer is 4 percent, I'm just going to buy stock that has a 4 percent dividend yield." But by now you've learned better—that kind of investment can inhibit your control over your income, potentially increase your taxes, and could hinder growth of your principal.

SUBTRACT YOUR DIVIDEND YIELD

We are going to take the required income percentage that we need, and we're going to subtract from that the dividend yield we're getting from your index fund. (Remember, because an index fund covers the whole market, some of the stocks it contains do pay dividends. We're minimizing our reliance on them.) If it's an S&P 500 fund, the dividend yield is currently about 2 percent, although that could certainly change up or down in the future.

So, if we need say four percentage points of income from the stock side, and our S&P 500 index fund pays 2 percent, what's left is a target of 2 percent for selling shares.

DIVIDE AND SELL!

Now we're going to apply our preferred frequency of selling

to that percentage. If we want to sell twice a year, and we need to sell 2 percent of the stock value, then each time we sell, it'll be 1 percent of the stock value.

A final word about the presence of dividends in your income mix: they will often be taxed as qualified dividends, at the same rate as long-term capital gains. As of 2020, if you're married and your income is below $80,000, you may be able to pay zero percent taxes on dividends and capital gains. If your income is higher, you may pay 15 percent or more. Everyone's tax situation is different, so contact your tax advisor for specific tax advice.

WORKING WITH AN ADVISOR

It's possible to do this on your own. But perhaps you're already working with an advisor, or would like to start. An advisor can make these calculations for you, and you can make them responsible for selling shares at whatever interval you both agree to.

I'm not advocating one approach over the other. It's a matter of preference. Would you rather learn what's required to do this yourself and spend the time doing it, or would you rather delegate the responsibility?

It's possible that your advisor won't be familiar with the income-on-demand strategy, or unclear whether it makes sense for your particular portfolio. My advice, literally, hand this book to your advisor, so that they can become familiar with it. Then you can discuss whether it's best for you and make an informed decision together.

Here's a question you should bring to that conversation: What stock holdings do I have that are focused on dividend production, and more importantly, which are lagging the S&P 500 over the long term? Remember, the returns of the S&P 500 represent an opportunity cost to you. You can invest in anything you want, but the S&P 500 returns are available to you at low cost and with plenty of diversification. In looking at the performance of your holdings compared to the S&P 500, you may be surprised by the answer and find there are substantial opportunities to make changes for the better.

A caution: As you talk with your advisor, be aware that they have likely been trained to offer dividend stocks or dividend-focused funds to clients who require income. If you want the benefits described in this book, the onus will be on you to ask for something different.

Your advisor should absolutely be able to accommodate. They might say that they can't do it or it's not part of their investment philosophy. If so, then you've got to decide whether your portfolio and your retirement is important enough for you to find a different advisor who can provide the benefits you're looking for.

PROTECT YOUR PRINCIPAL

When you embark on the sell-from-growth strategy I've laid out, it's helpful to make a record of your starting point—how much money is in the stock side of your portfolio from which you'll draw. That's your principal. Going forward, as you sell shares from your holdings, it's going to be helpful to know exactly where you are relative to where you started. Do you have more price appreciation available to draw from? Has a bear market brought you back to your starting point or below it?

Over time, as the market appreciates and your sales occur, the numbers in your brokerage firm statements will start to look a little muddied. The cost basis on your holdings is going to go down, and the unrealized gain amounts will change after share sales occur. That's okay. It's expected.

You can keep this simple by recording up front how much you started with in your index fund as you implemented this strategy. As the market appreciates, you're selling shares, and that's going to push the market value of your holding back closer towards its original value. That's exactly how this works. If you want to avoid selling from principal, just be sure your sales are not taking the dollar value of your holdings below its original principal amount.

There are times, of course, when the market falters. The sun's not always shining on the economy. In fact as I'm writing this, the market is down about 35 percent due to the coronavirus pandemic, making my next chapter especially relevant—how to handle tough times.

ENDURING A DOWN MARKET

MIKE TYSON, THE FAMOUS HEAVYWEIGHT BOXER-philosopher, was often asked what he expected his opponent to do when he stepped in the ring. "How is he going to fight you?" people would say.

His answer was as direct as a left jab. "Everyone has a plan until they get punched in the mouth," he'd reply. One day, late in his career, after Tyson himself had taken a few punches to the mouth, a reporter for the Ft. Lauderdale *Sun Sentinel* asked him to explain his thinking.

"What's going to happen?" he said. "Everybody has a plan until they get hit. Then, like a rat, they stop and freeze in fear." Here's where the philosopher in Tyson stood tall. "If you're good and your plan is working, somewhere during

ENDURING A DOWN MARKET · 115

the duration of that, the outcome of that event you're involved in, you're going to get the wrath, the bad end of the stick," he said. "Let's see how you deal with it. Normally people don't deal with it that well."

Of course, what's true in the ring is true outside of it too— at every stage of life, and certainly in retirement. Punches come. What matters is how you respond. If you choose to follow the growth-based, income-on-demand strategy I'm presenting, a punch might land as often as every two years.

According to an analysis of the S&P 500 by CNBC, since World War II we've seen twenty-five market corrections. A correction is defined as a drop of 10 percent or more. The average correction has seen a 13 percent market drop, and on average takes four months from the bottom to recover.

Bear Markets and Corrections - Historical Magnitude and Duration

Market Condition	Performance %	Length (months)	Recovery (months)
Bear Markets	-30	13.2	22
Corrections	-13	4.0	4

A bear market, on the other hand, is a drop of 20 percent or more in market value. We've seen thirteen of those since World War II. The average loss in market value is 30 percent. And the average duration: a bear market on average lasts thirteen months. That's how long it takes to go from market top to market bottom. The recovery on average takes twenty-two months. That means from the market bottom it takes roughly two years to get back to the top.

Put corrections and bear markets together and we've had thirty-seven "bad times" market punches in the mouth in the past seventy-four years.

TAKING THE PUNCH

Mike Tyson had it right. We need to be prepared. Every couple years, on average, we're going to have a down market; maybe it's going to last just a quarter; maybe it's going to last nearly two years. We've got to be ready for both.

Our goal is simple: avoid selling during a down market. Of course, you'll still need income during that time. We need to maintain a portfolio buffer—and in keeping with my theme of retirement castles, I call it a "cash moat." In my view, this cash amount should be able to cover at least four years of normal living expenses. That's the minimum, and it would leave little margin for error to cover an extreme market slump.

The worst of these we've seen since World War II may remain fresh in your thoughts—the Great Recession. From the time the market started dropping in 2008, it took four years for it to recover. That wasn't just a punch in the mouth; it was a wallop. A haymaker. Weathering that blow required a forty-eight-month cash moat.

I wouldn't stop there, either. I think of constructing portfolios the way an engineer would think of constructing a castle. We want to add in that margin of safety. I like to plan a five-year cash moat.

Could you get by with less? Yes, you could. But I'd contend that will make it harder to endure a down market psychologically. Your goal shouldn't be simply surviving a down market. Your state of mind shouldn't hinge on a quick recovery. It's your retirement; your goal should be enjoying every year, whether the market is up or down.

SIZING YOUR CASH MOAT

The first step in sizing your cash moat is to calculate your all-in annual spending. Your total budget. If you've got a financial plan, you know this figure already. Multiply that number by five, and you'll have a very healthy cash moat. You can make it bigger or smaller depending on your needs and preference.

I've had clients say to me, "Wait, JD, my budget isn't just one figure. There are the bills I need to pay, my groceries, gas for the car, taxes, medical bills. And there are discretionary expenses that come up every year—vacations, dinner out, a big ballgame. These I can control. The same goes for what I might call capital expenses—the new roof, the new car, refinishing the floors. During a down market, why not just cut back?"

That's a question I turn back at them. How would you like to turn to your spouse and say, "Honey, I know that we were planning on our dream vacation in six months, but because the market's down, we're putting that on hold. We didn't set aside enough in our cash moat." For most people, most of the time, their answer is that they do not want to have their retirement lifestyle interrupted by what the market's doing.

These are your golden years. You want to enjoy them. You could make a case for avoiding some capital expenditures, like a new roof. Perhaps you can wait another year on that. But everything that's important for enjoying your lifestyle, put it in your cash moat.

Conversely, I do want to stress this: it would be genuinely reckless to use the income-on-demand, sell-off strategy with no cash buffer in your portfolio. We are going to have market corrections, we are going to have bear markets, and you will not always be able to sell shares for profit. You are not being smarter if you implement this strategy without a cushion, or one that's too thin. You'd be taking on too much risk.

PUTTING SAFETY FIRST

Once we've determined how much to put in your cash moat, we need to decide where to put it. There are several options. One is to put one year's worth of spending in cash or a money market fund. The rest can go into laddered Certificates of Deposit, or CDs: a two-year CD, a three-year CD, a four-year year CD and so on. You can stagger those funds so that your money comes available as you need it.

Here's a second option if it suits you better: buy short-term, high-quality bonds instead. For example, if you could buy a US Treasury Note that matured within the time frame you need. Either way, when building your cash moat, it's best not to reach for yield. The whole point is safety.

CD OR MONEY MARKET FUND:

WHAT'S THE DIFFERENCE?

A Certificate of Deposit, or a CD, is issued by a bank and generally is insured by the federal government. A money market fund is essentially a fund created by your brokerage firm, which is responsible for generating the interest paid out on the fund by investing it. It does not have federal insurance. That said, money market funds are very safe; it was a big deal during the Great Recession when they dropped by as little as 1 percent, and there have been all kinds of measures put in place since to ensure that a drop even that small won't happen again.

You might find that CDs pay a slightly higher yield because you're locking up your money for a certain period of time. While a money market fund might pay a little less, you can sell it any time.

A third option for your cash moat, though not one I'd rank as highly, is a bond fund—but only if you ensure that the duration of the bond fund is very short. Duration is a measure of how sensitive a bond or a bond fund is to interest rate movement. The longer the maturity length, the higher the duration and the higher the sensitivity. By its nature, a bond fund will never mature; the managers will always keep pushing out its date of maturity. But a bond fund with high-duration holdings is more prone to fluctuations in price—and the whole point of the cash moat is having money there when you need it, without worry. If you do choose to buy a high-quality bond fund, a short-term fund is preferable.

RESTORING YOUR CASH MOAT

There will certainly be times when the market value of your index funds or your stocks drop below the original principal amount. That is normal, and that is okay. It's actually expected if we're utilizing a sell-off strategy, where we're constantly selling from growth and effectively dropping your portfolio back toward the original amount. When a market downturn takes that fluctuation below the original principal, that's when we put a pause on selling shares and instead make withdrawals from our five-year cash moat.

After the market recovers, we can resume selling shares. But now we'll have two purposes in mind. The first is to meet your income needs. The second is beginning to replenish what we've drawn from the five-year cash moat.

History suggests we'll get help from the dynamics of market recovery. Generally speaking, the greater the drop in the downturn, the greater the snapback in recovery. Again, let's take the Great Recession for example. It began in 2008; it took four years to regain the ground that was lost. And 2013 was a banner year for stocks, as the market surged by nearly 30 percent. Our income needs haven't changed by nearly that much, so we'll take advantage of that surge to replenish the five-year fund we've drawn down.

You need not replenish every dollar overnight. Take the Great Recession by way of example again. Having entered the recession with a five-year cash moat, we'd have emerged with one year left. If we had tried to replenish it all immediately in early 2013, as the market began its year of phenomenal growth, we'd have minimized the extent to which our index fund or stock holdings benefited. It would have been better to replenish it over two years, not just one. Below is a table of yearly returns of the S&P 500 over the past five decades. Note how strongly the market often rebounded following off-years—and how many more strong years there were than bad ones. (Of course, given the coronavirus pandemic, 2020 may be an off-year too. But the historical pattern is unmistakable.)

S&P 500 Total Return Percentage by Year

1970 - 1994

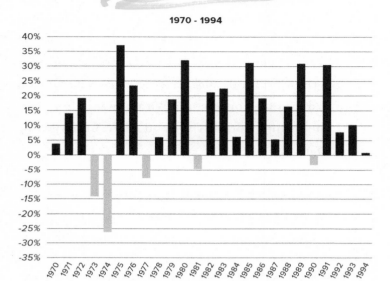

1995-2019

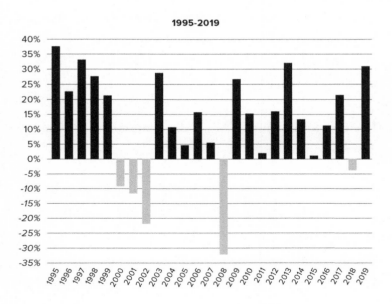

PUTTING IT IN WRITING

Jon Guyton is a well-known financial advisor based in Minneapolis: a retirement columnist for the *Journal of Financial Planning*, a contributor to money.com, and an expert panelist on retirement for the *Wall Street Journal*. And it's Guyton who introduced the concept of a Withdrawal Policy Statement to help guide both advisor and client in navigating a down market.

A Withdrawal Policy Statement is just what its name suggests: a formalized agreement, signed by all parties, that spells out what you're going to do when the market delivers that punch in the mouth. It's not a statement of strategies, but an actual action plan. When this happens, we'll do that. Rather than freezing or reacting to every turn in the new everyday—which can paralyze you—you can turn to a clear plan that defines where your income is going to come from, whether the market is up or down.

The first four elements of a policy statement that Guyton describes are:

1. The income goals your portfolio needs to support;
2. The assets available to meet those goals, including your cash moat;
3. The withdrawal rate needed to meet your goals; and
4. The method you'll use to determine the source of each year's withdrawal income.

I don't agree with everything Guyton advocates—most notably a mechanism for adjusting your spending down when the market is off, and up when it surges. As I've said, my preference is to structure your approach—and thus your policy statement—in a manner that doesn't require you to stop or slow your withdrawals in a down market. Neither do I believe you should automatically increase your withdrawals just because the market's going up. There's no reason to do either, just for the sake of doing it.

But it's essential to formalize your strategy for taking money out of your portfolio, up front, before the first punch lands. It needs to be written out—no shortcuts!

STAYING IN THE RING

If history shows that downturns come and recoveries follow, you might wonder this: Why not just step out of the ring before the punches start landing? Why not just jump out when the market turns sour, hold on to your assets while the market sinks, then jump back in when it begins to recover?

That was my Schwab client Robert's reaction in late 2018, when the market dropped from an all-time high by at least 10 percent from September to December, taking with it all the year's gains. You may remember it. Uncertainty over President Trump's trade tactics shook the markets. The pundits raised the specter of a new recession, and it seemed a plausible argument. After all, the economy's decade-long recovery from the Great Recession of 2008 couldn't last forever. Against the advice of our team at Schwab, Robert sold all the stock he held in his IRA and old 401(k) rather than risk more losses. "Look," he said, "with everything that's going on, the trade war and everything, I just don't think we can make money in stocks, at least for the next couple of years. So, I'm just going to hang out on the sidelines."

My response: "It's not about timing the market, it's about time *in* the market. It's important to stick to our long-term plan." We knew the history, and it was on Robert's side. The market would rebound and resume its growth; it was simply a question of when.

The answer was not long in coming. Starting at the beginning of 2019, the market rallied. The pundits scratched their heads. Robert stayed out. "Well," he said, "I see it's going up, but I'm going to wait until it falls back down to where I bought it in at and then I'll feel more comfortable getting back in."

Month by month, the market kept appreciating. By the end of 2019, the S&P 500 stood 30 percent higher than at the beginning of the year. At the time I left Schwab, Robert was just starting to agree to dollar-cost-averaging back into the market. He had slipped the punch—but he was paying the price for it. He still is. Because even if you guess right about when to jump out of the market, you also need to guess right about when to jump back in. You might as well take your money to the casino and try your luck there. It's easier than anticipating the market. And at least you'll have fun doing it.

The cautionary tale of Robert isn't all bad, because he was smart enough to leave his wife's holdings alone. And to her credit, she chose a different course. "I don't care what's going on in the market," Michelle told me when I called. "I know what's good for me." She held steady. As a result, she is dramatically outperforming her husband—because she stayed in the ring.

Yes, the market falls—more often than you might think. But it also comes back—more quickly than the pundits might suggest. Set aside your five-year cash moat and write your withdrawal policy. When the market's down, live by that policy. If you've crafted a policy that is right for you, you'll be able to stay in the ring longer than the pain of the market's punch.

ONE SIZE DOES NOT FIT ALL

In laying out this case—set aside a cash moat for the down times, put the rest of your portfolio in index funds and sell from growth when the market is up. I want to make one thing abundantly clear: This is not a one-size-fits-all proposition. This is not for everyone. The approach I'm recommending has worked very well for my clients in the past, and I am convinced it will continue to do so. But I also recognize that intelligent people may prefer to live with less portfolio fluctuation than the structure I recommend.

There's nothing wrong with that. You should do what makes sense for your own risk tolerance, and if having a portfolio with less stock makes sense to you, then you should do that. When I work with new clients, and they're weighing two stock allocations, one higher-stock allocation and the other lower, I prefer to start with the lower choice first. If you still have an appetite for more stocks when the market is down, then you've got the right temperament for it.

As an advisor, my job is to lay the groundwork for a client with a financial plan, because that tells them how much income they need, and then to show the range of returns they could generate. The decision of what balance to strike is the client's to make—and that's the case for you as a reader as well. Consider the case I'm making, consider your own circumstances and preferences, then make an informed decision. I simply want you to understand the consequences of your choice. And I want you to have a plan for that punch, because life tends to bring them, no matter what approach you take.

Having opened this chapter with a quote from boxer and philosopher Mike Tyson, I'll close by balancing him with E.A. Housman, an English scholar and poet who died in 1936—in the midst of the twentieth century's greatest economic punch of all, the Great Depression. Housman's words speak to a truth even deeper than the boxer's. May they guide you through times good and bad.

The thoughts of others
Were light and fleeting,
Of lovers' meeting
Or luck or fame.
Mine were of trouble,
And mine were steady;
So I was ready
When trouble came.

CHAPTER EIGHT

GAINING PEACE
OF MIND

SIR ISAAC NEWTON POSSESSED GREAT INTELLIGENCE and a remarkable capacity for insight. With his powers of observation and command of mathematics, he teased out the principles of physics that guided human understanding of the universe for centuries. He made sense of gravity, the tides, the paths of comets, built the first practical reflecting telescope, and developed a nuanced theory of color. He was a genius, one of the great scientists of all time.

And yet, when it came to the South Sea investment bubble, Newton was no different than anyone else. He succumbed to the emotions of the market, and he paid the price.

The South Sea Company was a private-public enterprise founded in Britain in 1711 and granted monopoly trading rights with South America. King George I himself became governor of the company; it took over the national debt and made unsustainable promises. Investors swallowed the bait, and the value of its stock soared more than eight times over.

Newton was among those investors, and he sensed the truth of the situation early on. All bubbles burst. He could, he wrote, "calculate the motion of the heavenly bodies but not the madness of the people." He dumped his shares, pocketing £7,000 and a 100 percent profit. It was a million-dollar win in today's money.

But the bubble kept getting bigger. Investor enthusiasm just kept growing. Newton couldn't help himself. He was missing out. He bought back in—at a much higher price.

When the company collapsed in 1720, the great thinker found himself out £20,000. That's about three million dollars today. According to Benjamin Graham, author of a book called *The Intelligent Investor*, "For the rest of his life he forbade anyone to speak the words 'South Sea' in his presence."

Ouch.

In enduring down markets and pursuing an income-from-growth strategy—and for that matter, to making the most of your retirement—it's essential to understand how important it is to prevent emotion from driving your decisions. That begins with understanding the role emotions can play when it comes to investing.

What happens when you ask a financial advisor for assurance in a down market? You probably get a technical response: "The Federal Reserve is lowering interest rates. The government is providing fiscal stimulus. The beta in your portfolio is low and we remain diversified."

If you're like me, answers like that aren't so helpful. That's because financial stresses bring out emotional responses. In this way, finance and psychology are linked together. Sometimes important financial questions require answers that address the emotions of the moment.

I have found that maintaining peace of mind in a down market is a matter of psychology, not finance. I advise my clients that there are four keys to managing the storm when it matters most:

1. View your stocks as a business, not a ticker symbol
2. Remember the parable of Mr. Market
3. Avoid checking stock prices
4. Maintain optimism

I'll get into each of these concepts in pages to come. But

first I want to step back and talk about why the emotions of a down market can be such a challenge to manage.

THE PSYCHOLOGY OF LOSS

There's a concept in psychology known as "loss aversion," and it helps explain why we react emotionally to stock prices. According to the website Decision Lab, this understanding of human behavior is grounded in findings published by two psychologists in 1992, demonstrating that people react differently to positive and negative changes in their status. A negative change, they found, was twice as powerful as a positive change. This explains, for example, why people buy insurance. They would rather agree to a small monthly loss—their payments—than face the risk, however small, of a bigger loss at some point in the future.

Charlie Munger, the vice chairman of Berkshire Hathaway, once wrote a book called *Poor Charlie's Almanac*, which was a spin on *Poor Richard's Almanac* by Ben Franklin. In it he told a story about the family dog, which illustrates a corollary of loss aversion that he called "Deprival Super-Reaction Syndrome."

The Mungers once owned a dog, he wrote, that was tame and good natured—unless you did one thing. If you tried to take food away from him after he already had it in his mouth, he'd bite. Simple as that. Every time. He couldn't help it. Now nothing could be more stupid, Munger wrote, than for a dog to bite his master. But that's what he'd do. He was a victim of Deprival Super-Reaction Syndrome.

How does this apply to investing?

Here's what I've observed: When we see our stocks appreciating in value, we keep checking our portfolio, we see the unrealized gain that we have, and the bigger that number gets the more comfortable we feel with it. "Okay," we think, "I've earned this profit and now it belongs to me." And then a bear market pops up and the gain gets ripped away. The feeling that comes from that is actually a worse psychological experience than if you would have never had that unrealized gain at all—and instead just been down slightly from when you bought in. Here's another way to put it: When it comes to profit, it's *not* better to have loved and lost than never to have loved at all.

And what does this mean for you? If you stop thinking of unrealized gains as belonging to you, it won't hurt as much if a bear market or correction takes them away. If you work to keep your emotions from rising too high when all seems rosy, it's easier to keep them from sinking too low when all seems dark.

Now let's get into the four keys to doing just that.

KEY 1: YOUR STOCKS AS YOUR BUSINESS

"Investing is most intelligent when it is most businesslike."

—BENJAMIN GRAHAM

I encourage my clients to think of their stock holdings not as a ticker symbol, bouncing up and down, but as a business they own. It's a small business, and it's generating wealth for you.

You bought your business because you believe in its long-term prospects. You measure the progress of your business through its profitability over time. You understand that some months, some years, will be better than others. If your business was a farm, you'd know there would be some years of drought and low yields—but also that there would be years of plenty too, and that over time, you're likely to get a good result.

So, what is so helpful about viewing stocks as a business? There are two major benefits. First, it sets your focus on what matters—long-term business results. This perspective gives you a set of metrics to evaluate your investment *separate from its daily trading price*. Wouldn't it be nice to know how your investment was performing separate from the daily ups and downs of the market? I'll discuss this more in a moment.

The second benefit is that it sets expectation in a way that allows you to be happier. Having worked directly with several hundred high net-worth families and interacting with thousands more who were managing their own money, I can tell you I constantly see investors chasing unrealistic expectations and become unhappy when they're not met. Perfectly intelligent people will ask for "Stocks with growth and income, but my portfolio value can't drop." Can you imagine owning a business and telling the CEO of your private business, "Grow this business, return capital to me, and make sure that nobody ever offers to buy my business for less than I paid for it." That's asking to control the uncontrollable.

If you're going to own stocks, which are fractional pieces of an operating business, you must be prepared for wild swings in price. I would argue if you're going to invest in the stock market at all you should be prepared to witness a 50 percent drop.

For a moment, imagine you own a private business. There is no price quote to check. How would we measure the performance of your business? In my view, we would want to measure two things:

First, the annual return on investment. This would be measured by how much profit the business earned for you relative to how much you have invested. As an example, let's say you invested $1 million into this business. Say that last year the company produced an after-tax profit of $50,000.

As the owner, your profit of $50,000 on an investment of $1 million represents a 5 percent rate of return. This 5 percent has nothing to do with stock price—this is a measure of business performance.

Second, we'd track the profit growth rate. If the business earned $50,000 last year, you'd probably like to see more profit this year. Let's say your business improves and you earn $53,000 this year. That means your business achieved profit growth of 6 percent. The significance of this growth rate is hard to overstate. It is widely followed and reported because in the long run, it determines changes in business valuation. Here's an example: from 1960 to 2018, the S&P 500 grew its profits by 6.7 percent annually. So how did the price of the S&P 500 change? It grew by 6.5 percent annually. Profit growth and price growth are tied together—whether that's upwards or downwards.

These same two metrics can be applied to your stock holdings—distinct from its current trading price. You can observe how much profit the companies produced on your behalf by taking the number of shares you own multiplied by the earnings per share. If you divide the resulting figure by how much you invested, you can see your return on investment. Second, you can look at the percentage growth in earnings per share. This allows you to track your profit growth rate.

Equipped with these tools, you can say goodbye to old thoughts like, "My stock is down 20 percent from where I bought last year. I made a terrible investment!" Instead, you can ask, "How has my investment performed from a business perspective?" This not only shifts your focus to the long term, it also makes your investing more businesslike.

What would this model of stocks-as-a-business look like if we applied it to owning a US index fund? You would own that fund because you believe in the long-term future of corporate America. You would measure progress by tracking the earnings growth of corporate America, which is to say its profitability over time. You would keep realistic expectations about the price of the index fund and the fundamentals of corporate America—understanding they will drop in value from time to time when we have a recession or, heaven forbid, even a depression. Finally, you would not check the price of your index fund every day or every week. Think of the time you'd save!

In the end, your portfolio is really just a tool for you to enjoy your life and your lifestyle. It's a means to an end. If you're checking it every day, you're focusing too much on the tool. It becomes more of a burden than a blessing. It means you're not spending time doing things that you enjoy with people you want to be with.

KEY 2: THE MR. MARKET PARABLE

In the opening of this chapter, I introduced you to Benjamin Graham and his book, *The Intelligent Investor*, which was published in 1949. At the heart of the book is what he called the Mr. Market parable.

Graham asked readers to think of the market quotations that are offered every day for individual stock prices, bond prices, mutual funds and so on, all those quotations, as being generated by a single man. His name is Mr. Market. And the unfortunate thing about him is that he's a manic depressive.

So some days he's pumped with optimism and he's going to offer higher and higher prices. Other days, sometimes for no good reason, he's downtrodden, pessimistic, and he's just going to offer lower and lower prices.

The point Graham made for investors with his parable is this: Mr. Market is there to serve you rather than to pressure you. If he's going to sell you stocks at cheap prices, it's on you to take advantage of them by buying. If he's going to offer to buy stocks at ultra-high prices, you should take advantage of them by selling.

What happens if you let Mr. Market pressure you?

Here's a way to think about that in the context of what,

for many middle Americans, is their largest investment in terms of equity: their home. Let's say we're talking about you, and you believe your home is worth $500,000.

Imagine Mr. Market knocking on your front door one day and saying, "Hi, I'd like to buy your home for $500,000." You say, "Thanks, but we really like our home, so we're going to have to decline and keep our house."

The next day there's another knock, knock, knock. "Hi," Mr. Market says, "I'd like to buy your home. And today, since you declined my offer yesterday, I'd like to offer $400,000." "No," you answer, "I still really like my home, and I'm not going to sell."

But in the back of your mind, you're now thinking, Well, the location isn't perfect and there was a burglary down the road last month. Maybe my home isn't worth as much.

Next day, knock, knock, knock. "Hi! I'd like to buy your home for $250,000."

Now the feeling is getting worse and you worry that the offers will just keep going lower. You think, "I don't want to wait until it's only worth $100,000. At least I could get out now for $250,000." And you sell your home for $250,000.

You might say that's silly, I would never sell my home just

because I was getting offered lower and lower prices. And yet people sell their stock holdings under these psychological circumstances all the time. When prices start falling, people start feeling like they're losing money, and it hurts. They stop believing their investment will make money over time and start believing it will lose money. They want the pain to go away, so they end up taking real losses in order to avoid larger potential losses.

The American presidential election in 2016 demonstrated this effect. The night of that election, the Dow futures dropped seven hundred points, which meant the market on the morning after would open substantially down from where it had been before. That spooked a number of people, including one of my clients, Tom, who thought he saw chaos coming and got out of the market altogether. I'm not arguing politics one way or another here; I'm talking about loss aversion, about fear. When you consider what the market did after that day, it's clear. Tom missed out on the gains to come.

When it comes to your portfolio, it can be a challenge to stand apart from the crowd and the emotions of the moment. I think bearing the Mr. Market parable is important. It helps you keep the market price of the moment in perspective. And you're less likely to feel the pressure of running with the crowd when negative emotions take hold.

KEY 3: AVOID CHECKING STOCK PRICES

The stock market is a tremendous reinforcement mechanism. Pick any stock you want. If the market continues to elevate the price of that stock higher and higher, you're going to feel better and better about your decision. And the opposite will be true, even more so, if the price is falling. The underlying long-term reasons for buying the stock won't matter nearly as much as the pain of the moment. Fear of loss can feed a powerful negative addiction, leading you to check the market constantly, which only breeds more anxiety. It's the financial equivalent of junk food. Once you start eating Doritos, it's hard to stop!

If you're constantly looking for validation of what you're doing, the easiest and quickest way to seek it is from the news. I once had a client named Allen who bought into the market when we began working together. A correction occurred several months later, and Allen decided to sell out on his own. It was loss aversion in action. He told me, "I'm going to wait for the news to get better before I get back in."

"The news is never going to tell you that this is the right time to get back in," I answered. It's never so positive as to assure you, without doubt, that now's the time. By its nature, the news is always framed to create at least some elements of uncertainty or doubt. By and large, it avoids optimism. And here's what that means for you. If you're waiting for the news to get to a point where you feel comfortable investing, that day will never come.

I once heard a talk that equated financial news with the Weather Channel. Forecasters are reluctant to say everything looks great here, nothing more to talk about. They'll say wind or rain may be coming, we'll have to see, maybe check back later. It's not actually there to teach you. The same is true of most financial news. It's there to stimulate you and get you hooked on watching.

THE NO-LOOK CHALLENGE

In the same way that golfers cannot make birdies by staring at the scorecard, investors cannot improve their returns by checking stock prices. Checking your portfolio constantly takes up more than a share of your time. It takes a share of your mind, especially when it becomes habit, because it distracts you throughout the day, especially when you start seeing patterns emerge. Hey, we've had three up days in a row! Will we get five? Vice versa—and then some—when it's down. Not again! What do I do? By eliminating that stress, my clients have found that they're more focused on things that they actually can control and that they actually want to get done.

Of course, breaking the habit of portfolio-checking can be easier said than done. I had a client named Susan.

She was a new investor who had received an inheritance. After we determined the right long-term portfolio, we decided to invest the money slowly over the course of a year. The amount we initially invested went down in trading price. It was off 5 percent or so by the time of our next meeting.

"These are big numbers," she said, "and the red is pretty significant there. I'm kind of worried about that."

My answer was what I called the No-Look Challenge. It's pretty simple: Ignore your portfolio balance for a while. Don't log in to your account. Leave it be.

"If you can go a quarter without checking the portfolio," I told her, "you'll win the challenge."

She took me up on it. Three months later she sent me a note. "Hey, I just realized we passed the quarter-long challenge!" she wrote. "Haven't checked it. Haven't worried about the market. I'm loving this whole new idea."

I sent her a bottle of wine with a message. "The best way to reduce stress is to not check the market," it said. "The second-best way is a glass of wine. Enjoy."

"If I knew doing nothing paid this handsomely," she replied, "I would have started sooner."

I'll close this section by presenting the same challenge to you. But I'll make it easier. Call it the one-month no-look challenge. If you're a long-term investor and your portfolio does not require changes, stop logging into your investment account every day. Remove the up-to-the-second stock quotes from your iPhone. Avoid watching the talking heads on financial television.

Define a reward upfront you'll give yourself for completing the challenge. Enjoy that reward at the end—you'll have earned it! And what's more, enjoy all the days in between.

KEY 4: MAINTAIN OPTIMISM

When I lay out my case for the sell-from-growth strategy, I'll sometimes get pushback from my own clients. "Yeah, I hear what you're saying," they'll say, "but this country's political division has never been worse, and plus, look at what's going on abroad right now."

If you're reading headlines it's easy to be pessimistic about the future. I'm not. I believe wholeheartedly that America will continue to prosper over time and that American business will continue to thrive. I don't mean to diminish the challenges and trials we face. We will continue to be confronted with economic recessions, natural disasters, pandemics, and wars. But our economy is based in a system of capitalism that, while not perfect, has produced incredible bounties and an improved standard of living far in excess of what we could have ever hoped for in 1776.

The foundation of capitalism is consumer demand for a higher standard of living over time—a better quality of life. Corporate America and small businesses everywhere strive to meet that demand. Crucially, capitalism and the profit motive give them the proper incentives for doing so. This is why just about every year we have access to improved foods, clothes, medicines, phones, transportation, entertainment—the list goes on. As companies continue to innovate for new products and services, and workers continue to increase their productivity per hour, companies generate higher profits. American business becomes more valuable and the virtuous cycle continues.

To appreciate just how far we've come, consider some of America's past titans of industry and what their fortunes afforded them versus what most Americans can afford today. Neither Vanderbilt, nor Carnegie, nor Rockefeller could have enjoyed the benefits of cheap internet access and the scope of humanity's knowledge that comes with it, cheap and convenient air travel across the globe, or the medical procedures and drugs that save countless lives today.

Consider the chart below from the Federal Reserve Bank of St. Louis. This chart shows the growth in real, per-capita Gross Domestic Product, or GDP, over time. GDP is a fancy-sounding term, but what it captures is straightforward: the value of goods and services that we produce in this country. By real, we mean adjusted for inflation. By per capita, we mean per person. What this adds up to is a fair proxy for the American standard of living.

Real Gross Domestic Product Per Capita

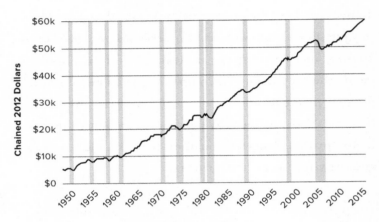

Shaded areas indicate US Recession

The charts take it from 1950, when real GDP per capita was $14,000 per person. Today, it's $58,000 per person. As a society, of course we still have work to do. But that represents a real gain of more than *four for one* in terms of improved standard of living. It means that Americans are living today far better than really at anytime in human history. Our access to food, housing, healthcare, transportation, entertainment—it's all improved dramatically over the last seventy years. That's only two generations.

Going forward, if our gains are even 2 percent per year, that means the next generation is going to have about twice the standard of living that we enjoy today. That's the power of compounded growth.

Not convinced? I'd encourage you to visit a website called usafacts.org. It was created by Steve Ballmer, who became employee number thirty at Microsoft in 1980 and went on to serve as the company's CEO for fifteen years. Since retiring in 2014, he has invested $2 billion in philanthropy, and is widely known now as the high-energy owner of the Los Angeles Clippers basketball team.

Ballmer's website is entirely based in data, stripped of political bias. It simply lays out the official, government-based numbers in a multitude of areas of public interest, from immigration to jobs to healthcare and trade and tariffs.

It's a phenomenal website. Not all the numbers are positive, but overall, I believe it documents the remarkable progress this country has made over time. Household net worth rose from $127,226 in 1980 to $728,765 in 2016. The homeless population nationwide fell by more than 25 percent between 2005 and 2017. Violent crime fell by 38 percent in the same period. Take a look at the following table from the United Nations' website regarding life historical and projected life expectancy in the USA.

Life Expectancy for the United States of America

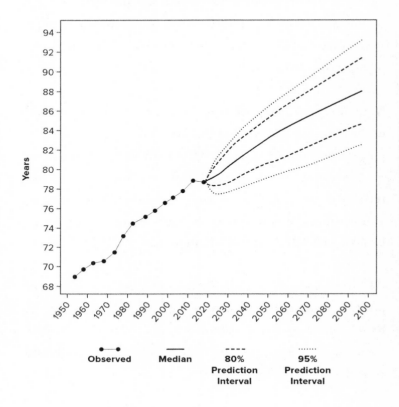

The progress isn't limited to our country alone, either. In his book, *Factfulness*, the late Hans Rosling, a Swedish global health professor, takes on what he characterizes as the myths that color our view of the world, rendering it far darker than it is. The book opens with a quiz that lays bare what he called the negativity bias in our understanding. Take a guess at the answer to one of his questions. Has the number of people living in extreme poverty worldwide over the last twenty years doubled, stayed the same, or been cut in half?

It's been cut in half.

You can find a version of the quiz on gapminder.org, the website Rosling established to present the data that make this case: ours is a world where most things improve, a world that is not divided, a world that, while far from perfect, has never been "less bad."

"Almost nobody knows the basic global facts!" the home page declares.

Nick Murray, a well-known author on financial matters, has an important statement on optimism worth sharing: "Optimism is the only long-term realism. Optimism is the only worldview that squares with the historical record."

Whether you realize it or not, even the status quo, play-it-safe approach of a retirement portfolio based in dividend-paying stocks for income is an expression of optimism. Those investors are still choosing a company that they expect to become more profitable over time. The difference is, rather than getting income by selling shares, they've chosen to get it by taking dividends. From a philosophical point of view, there's not much difference between the old, conventional approach of dividend-paying stocks versus the index fund growth strategy I've outlined. All that's really changing is the mechanics of how you take income.

So, if you've invested in the market, whether you realize it or not, you're an optimist. Welcome to the club!

IF YOU REMEMBER ONE THING...

Having peace of mind while holding stocks is achievable if you focus on the four keys: think of your stocks as a business, remember the parable of Mr. Market, avoid checking stock prices, and stay optimistic.

CONCLUSION

If you can dream—and not make dreams your master;
If you can think—and not make thoughts your aim;
If you can meet with Triumph and Disaster
And treat those two impostors just the same ...
If you can fill the unforgiving minute
With sixty seconds' worth of distance run,
Yours is the Earth and everything that's in it...

FROM THE POEM *IF*, BY RUDYARD KIPLING

CHARLIE MUNGER IS AN INTELLECTUAL HERO OF MINE.
The wisdom he shares in the pages of his *Poor Charlie's Almanac*
influences my approach to everyday life. Munger is nine-
ty-six now, and when I have a chance to hear him speak, I
don't miss it.

Munger is the chairman of the Daily Journal Corporation,
a small legal publishing business in Los Angeles. Every

year right around Valentine's Day, the company holds a stockholder meeting at which Munger delivers remarks and takes questions. I've been attending for the past five years, and I've had the opportunity to ask him a few questions and talk a little bit. At the Daily Journal meeting in 2020, I asked him his thoughts on the approach I've advocated through this book. Does it make sense for investors, I asked, to put their money in an index fund and take the income they need by selling from growth?

"I think the reason that it's growing is that for most people it does work better," he answered. Then he addressed human nature. "On the other hand," he said, "there's a huge proclivity to gamble. It's very interesting to play in a game where the returns are variable...

"In China, the ordinary holding period for the individual [who owns stocks] is very short," he continued. "They like to gamble in stocks. This is really stupid. It's hard to imagine anything dumber than the way the Chinese will hold stocks. They're so good at everything else.

"It shows how hard it is to be rational."

He's right, of course. It is hard to be rational. It's easy to let your hopes—or your fears—drive your decisions.

My hope for this book is that it's made it easier for you to be rational about funding your retirement. It's not always easy, but by the same token, it is always achievable. I have no doubt that it's vitally important to your financial well-being in the years to come. I believe that the facts I've outlined support the "Income on Demand" case I've made. I hope I've demonstrated that:

- The conventional, dividend-based approach to funding retirement potentially leaves you with less control over your income, higher taxes, and a portfolio that is likely to underperform the market;
- A total return, income-on-demand approach gives you more control over your income while potentially reducing your taxes;
- The foundation for this approach is a financial plan that identifies how you can meet your financial goals in a way that works for you;
- A passive investment strategy based on building your portfolio around an index fund is almost certain to deliver better results versus active portfolio management over time;
- Where you place your assets and the order in which you draw from them can help lower your lifetime taxes and those of your heirs;
- In years of growth, you can meet your income needs by selling shares at scheduled intervals;
- In off years, you can protect your principal by drawing on a cash moat instead; and

- Thinking of your holdings as a business rather than a ticker can free you from the addictive and emotional mood swings of the market.

All that said, I'm not advocating a one-size-fits-all, take-it-or-leave-it approach. I think of knowledge as power, and I want you to make informed decisions—your own decisions. I hope I've encouraged you to ask your own questions, your own "whys," as I did, and to seek your own answers. I hope you'll consider the case I've made and take from it as much—or as little—as makes sense to you. I also hope you'll be what Charlie Munger would call a "rational thinker" about your choices, and that I have helped you understand those choices in a new and better way.

You have worked hard to position yourself for retirement. I want you to move forward into this phase of life with confidence. The decisions are yours to make, and the retirement years are yours to enjoy. You've earned that much, and more!

ACKNOWLEDGMENTS

WARREN BUFFETT AND CHARLIE MUNGER—THANK YOU
to the best teachers I never had. You taught me more about
investing than any book, industry license, or professional
designation. You gave me a love for lifelong learning, without which I'd be hopping around like a one-legged man in
an ass-kicking contest.

Mark Travis—I'm afraid to think about how this book would
have turned out without your help and expertise. Thank
you for making this book an enjoyable process and for your
friendship along the way.

Emily Anderson—Thank you for caring as deeply about
the quality of this book as I do, and for keeping the whole
team organized.

John Barron of Apollo Coaching—Thank you for helping me set the foundation of my firm and message to the world. Thank you for the lesson on showing a reader how to interact with a message, and for the continuing advice and support.

The Junto—Thanks, gents, for your help and feedback. May something in this book count toward our next segment of, "Tell me something I don't know."

Michael Kitces—Thank you for the insightful content you bring to your blog on a consistent basis. The idea of writing a book in the first place came from a guest blog post.

Travis Bradberry—Thank you for sharing your insights and encouraging me to hustle.

Corey Wiederholt, CPA, CFP®—Thank you for your tax expertise and helping ensure accuracy in this book.

And finally, to all my family, friends, and clients at Farnam who encouraged me and supported me through the development.

I am grateful.

DISCLOSURES

Farnam Financial ("Farnam") is a registered investment advisor offering advisory services in the State of Arizona and in other jurisdictions where exempted. Registration does not imply a certain level of skill or training.

This publication is for informational purposes only and is not intended as tax, accounting, or legal advice, as an offer or solicitation of an offer to buy or sell, or as an endorsement of any company, security, fund, or other securities or non-securities offering. This publication should not be relied upon as the sole factor in an investment-making decision.

Past performance is no indication of future results. Investment in securities involves significant risk and has the potential for partial or complete loss of funds invested. It should not be assumed that any recommendations made by the Author, in the future, will be profitable or equal the performance noted in this publication.

The holdings identified do not represent all of the securities purchased, sold, or recommended for advisory clients of Farnam, and the reader should not assume that investments in the securities identified and discussed were or will be profitable.

One cannot invest directly in an index.

Limitations inherent in model results: Model portfolios, charts and other information presented do not represent actual funded trades and are not actual funded portfolios. As a matter of important disclosure regarding the model results presented, the following factors must be considered when evaluating the long- and short-term performance figures:

Historical or illustrated results presented herein do not necessarily indicate future performance. Investment in securities involves significant risk and has the potential for partial or complete loss of funds invested.

The results presented may have been generated during a period of mixed (improving and deteriorating) economic conditions in the US and positive and negative market performance. There can be no assurance that these favorable market conditions will occur again in the future.

The back-tested performance was derived from the application of a model with the benefit of hindsight.

The results portrayed reflect the reinvestment of dividends and other income.

The performance results presented are from a model portfolio, not an actually funded portfolio, and may not reflect the impact that material economic and market factors might have had on the advisor's decision making if the advisor were actually managing clients' money, and thus present returns which are greater than what a potential investor would have experienced for the time period. The results are presented for informational purposes only. No real money has been invested in this model portfolio. The model performance results should be considered mere "paper" or pro forma performance results. The model results do not represent actual funded trades and may not reflect actual prices paid or received for actual funded trades.

In some cases, clients had investment results materially lower than the results portrayed in the model.

This publication contains statements that are, or may be considered to be, forward-looking statements. All statements that are not historical facts, including statements about our beliefs or expectations, are "forward-looking statements" within the meaning of The US Private Securities Litigation Reform Act of 1995. These statements may be identified by such forward-looking terminology as "expect," "estimate," "plan," "intend," "believe," "anticipate," "may," "will," "should," "could," "continue," "project," or similar statements or variations of such terms. Our forward-looking statements are based on a series of expectations, assumptions, and projections, are not guarantees of future results or performance, and may involve substantial risks and uncertainty. All of our forward-looking statements are as of the date of this report only. We can give no assurance that such expectations or forward-looking statements will prove to be correct. Actual results may differ materially. You are urged to carefully consider all such factors.

All opinions and estimates constitute Farnam's judgment as of the date the information was printed and are subject to change without notice. Farnam does not warrant that the information will be free from error. The information should not be relied upon for purposes of transacting securities or other investments. Your use of the information is at your sole risk. Under no circumstances shall Farnam be liable for any direct, indirect, special, or consequential damages that result from the use of, or the inability to use, the information provided herein, even if Farnam or a Farnam authorized representative has been advised of the possibility of such damages.

The information herein is provided "AS IS" and without warranties of any kind either express or implied. To the fullest extent permissible pursuant to applicable laws, Farnam Financial LLC (referred to as "Farnam") disclaims all warranties, express or implied, including, but not limited to, implied warranties of merchantability, noninfringement, and suitability for a particular purpose.

Federal tax advice disclaimer: As required by US Treasury Regulations, you are informed that, to the extent this presentation includes any federal tax advice, the presentation is not written by Farnam to be used, and cannot be used, for the purpose of avoiding federal tax penalties. Use of any information presented by Farnam is for general information only and does not represent individualized tax advice, either express or implied. You are encouraged to seek professional tax advice for income tax questions and assistance.

ABOUT THE AUTHOR

JONATHAN BIRD was born in Phoenix, Arizona. He graduated from Creighton University with a BA in Philosophy. He worked for Charles Schwab for six years and managed more than $250 million in client assets. He holds both the Certified Financial Planner™ and Certified Wealth Strategist® designations. In 2019 he founded Farnam Financial to begin his mission of accelerating society's shift towards passive stock ownership and providing clients with peace of mind through all markets. Farnam Financial is an independent Registered Investment Advisory firm and is proud to serve as a fiduciary to clients.

Outside of work Jonathan enjoys running a Junto group inspired by Benjamin Franklin's autobiography. He also enjoys reading nonfiction, playing golf, and pickleball.

Jonathan can be reached by email at jonathan@farnamfinancial.com or at www.farnamfinancial.com.

Made in the USA
Las Vegas, NV
24 September 2021